THE

BLACK

KEYS

THE BIOGRAPHY

BY NICK THOMAS

GEM EDITIONS

ISBN: 978-1735152318

Library of Congress Cataloging-in-Publication Data

Thomas, Nick
     The Black Keys: The Biography
     Includes bibliographical references
     ISBN 978-1735152318

     1. Rock music – Ohio. 2. Rock music – History and criticism. 3. Rock music – Bio-bibliography.
     I. Title

Please contact the publisher to report any errors or omissions. Organizations and other groups interested in purchasing quantities of this book should contact the publisher.

This is not an official or authorized work. The Black Keys, their record companies, their managers and their representatives did not participate in the writing, editing, production or publication of this book.

Cover photo credit: imagepressagency / depositphotos.com

Printed in the U.S.A.

▶ TABLE OF CONTENTS

▶ INTRODUCTION

The Black Keys emerged from the Midwestern city of Akron, Ohio, which took its name from the Acropolis, a majestic landmark in Athens, Greece. Situated just 45-miles south of Cleveland, Akron was the highest point on the Ohio & Erie Canal, which by 1832 had connected Lake Erie to the Ohio River. Akron quickly grew around the 21 hand-operated locks that raised and lowered the canal's water level, which allowed shipping boats to proceed. With the process of passing through the city taking a full six-hours, the crews of these vessels had time to unwind, visit taverns and spend money.

From its humble beginnings as a canal town, Akron emerged as an industrial center whose growth was tied to advances in transportation. With the rise of the automobile industry at the start of the 20th century, the city became a boomtown. From 1910 to 1920, Akron was the fastest-growing city in the entire nation as the city's population tripled to 208,000.

Akron was transformed into the Rubber Capital of the World, as virtually every major American tiremaker was

1

headquartered in the city. For more than eight-decades, auto and truck tires were produced in Akron by companies such as Goodyear, Goodrich, General, Firestone, Seiberling and Mohawk. At one point, nearly two-thirds of all tires sold in the U.S. were manufactured in the city.

Much of the city's workforce had migrated from the Appalachian hills of West Virginia and western Pennsylvania. Many workers were first-generation immigrants from the countries of Eastern Europe. The smoke-belching factories even lured future actor Clark Gable, who earned $95 per week. Workers lived in neighborhoods that were named Goodyear Heights and Firestone Park, while their children attended Goodrich Junior High and Firestone High. And as fortunes were made, graceful mansions and grand estates were built on the city's northwest side.

In celebration of the charcoal-colored compound essential too tire-making, Akron was nicknamed the Rubber City. The local college football team played their games at the Rubber Bowl. In the 1930s, Akron was also home to an annual formal gala, the Rubber Ball, which was staged in the aptly named Rubber Room nightclub, located in the Portage Hotel. The glitzy affair attracted the city's movers and shakers who dressed in elaborate outfits made completely out of rubber.

The city was also the birthplace of Alcoholics Anonymous and the one-time home of Civil War-era abolitionist John Brown. And despite the claims from two other cities, Akron is also considered the birthplace of the hamburger. In 1885, when Akron restaurateur Charles Munches set up a booth at the Erie Agricultural Fair in Hamburg, New York, he introduced the soon-to-be beloved hamburger, 75-years before Ray Crock began expanding McDonald's into an international chain.

By the 1950s, Akron offered a comfortable slice of postwar middle America. With the emergence of car culture and the construction of a national interstate highway system, the demand for tires remained strong. The city was home to numerous drive-in theaters, bowling alleys, roller rinks, drive-in restaurants and a popular amusement park with roller coasters and a large bandstand that featured musical acts and offered plenty of room for dancing, Summit Beach Park. A bustling downtown boasted two large department stores that proudly faced each other on the same street. The city also embraced fine arts with the world class Akron Art Museum and a local orchestra.

Later, Akron's neighbor, Cleveland, was later selected as the site of the Rock and Roll Hall of Fame. The museum was built in the city, in large part, due to pioneering deejay Alan Freed, who worked behind the microphone at radio stations in both Akron and Cleveland.

Raised in Salem, about an hour east of Akron, Freed was credited with popularizing the term "rock and roll." After a series of radio jobs, including as the host of a classical music show in nearby Youngstown, he was hired in 1945 by WAKR in Akron, whose studio was situated in the basement of the city's tallest building. At the station, Freed played contemporary pop music for the first time in his career. Initially hired as a news reporter, he was given his own show after the scheduled announcer had called off. With Freed emerging as a local media star, his salary tripled in just two-years. Amassing a loyal following of teens and young adults, he set local ratings records in Akron.

Alan Freed at WAKR in Akron, 1949.

Terminated in 1950 after demanding one too many raises, Freed was immediately hired by a competing Akron station that was located across the street from WAKR. However, he was forced to quit after just one day behind the microphone when his former employer enforced the terms of his employment contract.

Freed returned to the radio airwaves in June 1951 at WJW in Cleveland as the host of an overnight classical music show. During this period, deejays were permitted to select the music they played. On the advice of close friend Leo Mintz, Freed started playing R&B, blues and doo-wop music. Mintz had observed a new trend of white teenagers requesting records by contemporary black artists at his busy, downtown Cleveland store, Record Rendezvous. With Freed naming his radio show, *The Moondog Rock And Roll House Party*, he dominated the Cleveland-Akron airwaves.

In 1954, Freed was lured to a radio station in New York City. Working at WINS, he emerged as the most powerful deejay of the decade and often overshadowed the music he played. Continuing his concert promotions on a national level, Freed toured with the top acts of the day. He also embarked on a two-year residency at New York's Paramount Theater and earned millions with his all-star revues, breaking attendance records that had been set a decade earlier by Frank Sinatra. Freed expanded his rock kingdom to include films and a syndicated radio show. He also hosted a television show on ABC – the first-ever network rock and roll program – which predated *American Bandstand*.

Meanwhile, Freed's replacement at WAKR in Akron, Scott Muni, was later a major player in the rise of the progressive rock format in New York City. Another employee at the station, receptionist Lola Albright, also enjoyed success in the entertainment field. After playing a nightclub singer on the popular television series, *Peter Gunn*, she scored a co-starring role opposite Elvis Presley in the film, *Kid Galahad*. Another announcer at WAKR, Art Fleming (then known as Art Fazzin) later hosted the first run of the classic game show, *Jeopardy!*

During the 1960s, Akron would produce only a few nationally known musical acts, most notably Ruby & The Romantics, who topped the pop charts with "Our Day Will Come." Another local group, Jordan Christopher & The Wild Ones, recorded the first version of the garage-rock classic, "Wild Thing," a year before the Troggs released the definitive rendition of the song.

Following a devastating rubber workers' strike in the late-1970s, Akron lost most of its economic cornerstones. Over a several-year period ending in 1982, all of Akron's big rubber factories stopped producing passenger tires. As writer Russ Musarra observed: "Employment in Akron rubber companies, once at 60,000, was 28,453 in 1976 after a four-month strike, longest in the industry's history. By 1982, plant closings had reduced employment to 17,366."

The huge loss in the number of good-paying factory jobs would also devastate other businesses in the city. Downtown's two majestic department stores – Polsky's and O'Neil's – would soon shutter their doors. Even the city's fabled downtown record store, Edfred's, closed down in 1978 after 64-years in business.

From this post-industrial landscape of abandoned factories all across the Midwest, a new term emerged – the Rust Belt. Local musician Brad Warner recalled: "One of my clearest memories of Akron from when I used to go there with my dad from the suburbs where we lived is the smell. As soon as you crossed the city limits, it was like you were breathing the fumes of a million tires. The perpetually cloudy skies turned a shade grayer from the tons of smoke Firestone, Goodyear, Goodrich and Seiberling constantly pumped into the air. By the time I graduated high school in 1982, that smell was already a thing of the past."

Likewise, LeBron James said of his hometown: "If you went high up on North Hill in the 1980s, you could tell that life was not like it once was: the obsolete smokestacks in the distance, the downtown felt so tired and weary. I won't deny it – there was something painful about all of that."

Dan Auerbach observed: "It's kind of a strange little town. It's got all these ghosts of the past lurking around every corner, these giant buildings, old mansions everywhere. Empty factory buildings. Turn of the century Akron was just poppin' like crazy. Some of the richest people in North America were living there and had mansions. And then all of that went away!"

Although the local economy was decaying and the region's population was shrinking, there was still a strong art and music scene in Akron. In the wake of Devo's success in the late-1970s, an increasing number of bands performed original music. In nightclubs such as the Crypt and the Bank, pioneering punk and new wave bands – Tin Huey, the Rubber City Rebels, Hammer Damage, the Bizarros, the Waitresses and Chi-Pig – were originators of what was soon dubbed the Akron Sound.

Ralph Carney – who got his start in Tin Huey and later worked with the B-52's and Tom Waits – observed: "I think it was all the rubber dust we inhaled. I think there are similar scenes in many industrial towns like Detroit but in Akron, there definitely was an unusual amount of weird bands. When you're in a place like Akron, you make up your own reality of what you want to play." Chrissie Hynde, meanwhile, left Akron for London and had great success as the leader of the Pretenders.

*   *   *   *   *   *

Although Ohio is far removed from the Delta region of Mississippi – the birthplace of the blues — the music has flourished throughout the Buckeye State, particularly in areas with large populations of African-Americans such as Cincinnati and Cleveland. Additionally, the Cincinnati-based label, King Records, churned out hits by dozens of notable R&B and blues acts such as James Brown, Memphis Slim and Little Willie John. Another artist at the label, Cleveland-born blues shouter Bull Moose Jackson, scored a string of chart hits.

In the years after World War II, African-Americans migrated from the South to work in the many smoke-belching auto, steel and tire factories across Northeastern Ohio. A host of nightclubs accommodated the influx, including Lindsay's Sky Bar, the Theatrical Grill and Gleason's. Touring African-American musicians usually stayed at the Majestic Hotel, which also housed a jazz club. In the years before the rise of R&B and rock and roll, danceable hot jazz and electric blues dominated the local scene.

Cleveland nurtured a number of talented blues players. Guitarist Robert Lockwood Jr. was a fixture on the city's musical landscape for decades. Called the last living link to legendary guitarist Robert Johnson, Lockwood received musical training as a child from his stepfather. Following the poisoning death of Johnson in 1938, Lockwood played behind Sonny Boy Williamson on the popular radio show, *The King Biscuit Time*. Landing in Chicago during the 1950s, Lockwood worked as a session player at Chess Records behind some of the city's finest blues players, including Sunnyland Slim, Eddie

Sarah's on South Main Street in downtown Akron.

Boyd and Little Walter.

But with the popularity of blues waning in the early-1960s, Lockwood settled in Cleveland and raised a family. At the time, the local blues scene was in decline. In the ensuing years, Lockwood emerged as a musical institution in Cleveland. Frequently performing around the city, the Grammy-nominated bluesman held down a weekly residency at Fat Fish Blue. In the late-1980s, he befriended a transplanted British slide-guitarist named Mr. Downchild, who made the city his home. Another local bluesman, Bill Miller – better known as Mr. Stress – was celebrated in Chrissie Hynde's musical ode to the city of Cleveland, "Precious."

Akron also enjoyed its own blues tradition, although not a huge one. In the 1940s and '50s, Howard Street – at the northern edge of the downtown district – was home to dozens of black-owned businesses. Inside the Hotel Matthews, a popular nightclub drew the finest in R&B, jazz and blues, including Duke Ellington, Cab Calloway, Ella Fitzgerald and Ray Charles. Sadly, the entire district was bulldozed in the 1960s as part of an urban renewal project.

Two decades later, it took a former professional football player to bring blues music back to downtown Akron. While storefront after storefront along South Main Street was boarded up, Al Kerkian – who was drafted by the Dallas Cowboys in 1967 – demonstrated to city leaders that Akronites would come downtown for nightlife if offered the opportunity. In 1981, Kerkian converted a two-story, former fast-food restaurant into a popular blues and jazz club – Sarah's Deli, which was named after his young daughter. Packed on weekends, the venue hosted local favorites such as the Baseliners, the Howard Street Blues Band and the Numbers Band.

A mainstay in the Akron/Kent area for more than fifty-years, the Numbers Band was launched in 1970 by brothers Robert and Jack Kidney during the wake of the Kent State shootings. The group also included Terry Hynde (the brother of Chrissie Hynde) and, for a time, Chris Butler of the Waitresses and Jerry Casale of Devo.

*   *   *   *   *   *

Emerging from a basement in Akron, Ohio, the Black Keys took the music world by storm by blending traditional electric blues with modern indie-styled rock. A minimalist, stripped-down, high-energy, two-piece act, the Black Keys quickly amassed a loyal fanbase shortly after the start of the new millennium.

Formed by singer-guitarist Dan Auerbach and drummer Patrick Carney, the duo recorded their earliest albums in a makeshift studio that was set up between a washing machine and a furnace. Carney, who was eleven-months younger than Auerbach, recalled that the pair connected through their shared love of the blues: "Dan and me grew up five or six doors down from each other, but we never hung out except for trading baseball cards. We thought we had nothing in common. He was a long-haired, pot-smoking soccer player, and I was a... Devo fan, but in late high school we found out we were both into R.L. Burnside."

Carney attributed the formation of the Black Keys to his upbringing in Ohio: "Akron had the perfect recipe for a young person to find themselves getting into music. When we were teenagers, we didn't have the internet. We didn't have much to do. And the weather was pretty horrible from basically November through March, and getting into the basement and playing music was the only thing my friends and I would do."

▶ CHAPTER 1
PATRICK CARNEY

Patrick James Carney was born in Akron on April 15, 1980. He had three brothers. While his father, Jim, was a reporter for *The Akron Beacon Journal*, his mother, Mary Stormer, worked as a real estate agent and was a prominent member of the Akron Board of Education. Carney's aunt, Elinore Marsh Stormer, was a local judge. (She would later help the Black Keys decipher their first record contract.)

Carney's first musical memory occurred at age three, when he heard "Electric Avenue" by Eddy Grant. The catchy, synth-heavy song would stick with Carney for the rest of his life. At age five, a photo of an unsmiling Carney appeared in an *Akron Beacon Journal* article about back-to-school fashions. The caption read: "Patrick Carney, 5, in stonewashed denim vest and trousers and coordinating shirt." His parents divorced the following year, when he was six.

Reared in a musical family, Carney was encouraged to pursue creative endeavors. His uncle, Ralph Carney, played the saxophone in the popular Akron new wave band, Tin Huey. The younger Carney recalled: "We would go spend the night at my grandparents' house every Friday, and my grandma would put on the Tin Huey record. It melted into my brain – it was my favorite record as a kid." Carney displayed mature musical tastes at a young age and came upon another album that would shape his musical outlook: "When I was about seven or eight, this record showed up... Tom Waits' *Rain Dogs*. I was very confused by it; the music is scary, but I listened to it incessantly."

In 1989, Carney met his future bandmate, Dan Auerbach. Carney recalled: "My father moved into Dan's neighborhood when I was 9. We got a house a couple houses down from where Dan lived. We didn't know each other superwell, but we'd ride bikes." Later, Carney would occasionally play tag football with Auerbach and his friends. Carney recalled that he tried to "fit in a little bit with the older kids in the neighborhood. I would purposefully do one-sided baseball card deals not in my favor just to try to hang out with these dudes."

At age ten, Carney purchased his first single – "Ice Ice Baby" by white rapper, Vanilla Ice. His father was horrified by the song. The younger Carney recalled: "My dad was like, 'This is absolute trash...' Right then he took it upon himself to start righting the ship, and... he bought me *Freak Out!* by" Frank Zappa.

Wanting to learn how to play the songs he would hear on his father's stereo, Carney recalled: "By the time I was 12 years old... I asked for a guitar, and my dad got me an electric Cort. The next thing I asked for was a Tascam Porta 02... and my dad got it for me for Christmas the next year. I mowed the lawn and did chores just so I could get an ART reverb. I was obsessed."

During the grunge era of the early-1990s, Carney desperately wanted a guitar like the one played by his musical idol, Kurt Cobain. Spotting a 1964 Daphne Blue Fender Mustang in the classified section of *The Akron Beacon Journal*, Carney's father purchased the instrument for his son. (Just weeks later, Cobain would end his own life.)

Continuing to immerse himself in music, Carney was curious about his father's extensive record collection and decided to alphabetize the albums: "I just wanted to see what was there. It took me four or five hours... I didn't understand all the folky stuff."

While attending junior high school, Carney began playing music with some of his classmates. He later recalled: "I wasn't very good at guitar, so I couldn't really play along with anything. When I was 14, me and my friends thought we were like Sonic Youth. We'd let our guitars feed back and think we were really cool. And we'd change the name of the band every week.... Then we had a band called the Deprogrammers – that was our fake-jazz outfit. We never played live, but if we ever did, we were going to dress up as what we thought jazz musicians would dress like."

Also that year, Carney joined his father for an out-of-state Easter Break visit to the home of a family friend. In the basement, Carney discovered an old Ludwig drum kit. Spending most of the visit trying to play the drums, he was enamored with the instrument.

Carney wanted to find a job in order to buy some more musical gear. Making a deal with his mother, he agreed to save half of his earnings and was permitted to spend the rest on whatever he wanted. He recalled: "When I was 15, I lied about my age and I got a job washing dishes. I started buying everything I thought you needed to be a band." Setting up the equipment in his father's basement – including a drum kit, guitar and mixing board – Carney often jammed with friends. However, none of them were impressed by his skills on the guitar.

During this time, Carney became a huge fan of Devo. He has often cited their debut, *Q: Are We Not Men? A: We Are Devo!*, as one of his top-five albums. Carney and his friends would often lurk outside of the home of Robert Mothersbaugh, Sr. – better known to Devo fans as General Boy – to catch a glimpse of the father of Bob and Mark Mothersbaugh.

Carney was also influenced by a three-piece band that combined punk, garage rock and blues: "I was obsessed with the Jon Spencer Blues Explosion right when I was 15, when that record *Orange* came out. I had a band in high school with my two friends, and it was two guitars and drums. And for a long time, to be honest, I guess I didn't understand the importance of bass until I was probably in my mid-20s. It was the indie rock thing... just to have an unusual lineup. I don't really know why." That year, Carney and his two bandmates played their first-ever public gig at the Mantis on North Water Street in Kent. The informal, dimly lit, run-down art gallery and music venue was home to a number of underground punk and indie rock groups. The underage Carney was driven to the gig by his father.

Around this time, Pat and his uncle, Ralph Carney, went guitar shopping at a number of Akron-area pawn shops. Pat Carney recalled: "When I was 16, I visited him when he was living in San Francisco and he introduced me to the weirdest kinds of music, the most esoteric." The older Carney remembered: "It was totally great. I remember thinking 'this guy is into the weird.' I played him wacky children's records from the '60s, turned him onto the Shags. Stuff that was primitive... outsider music." Over the years, the two men would remain close.

However, Pat Carney's musical career almost ended before it even started after he had an unfortunate accident while prepping food with a knife at a health food market just outside of Akron. As he recalled: "I was 16, but I was able to use the knife because I lied about my age. They thought I was older than I really was. This guy walks up and shows me this little catalog of people.... What the hell? I kept chopping with the knife and cut my... pinky off! I didn't even realize I'd done it. So the guy grabs some duct tape and tapes my finger back. Of course he does, he's a punk rock dude. They fix everything with duct tape." Carney made his way to an emergency room, where his finger was surgically reattached – without duct tape. As a result of the injury, he lost some feeling in the finger, which forced him to briefly give up playing the guitar.

▶ CHAPTER 2
CARNEY PICKS UP A GUITAR

Pat Carney attended Harvey S. Firestone High School, which was located in Akron's more affluent northwest side. The school would produce a number of notable alumni, including model Angie Everhart, astronaut Judith Resnick, Olympic gold medalist Mark Gangloff and actress Melina Kanakaredes. In the field of music, the list included singer-songwriter Joseph Arthur (who dropped out before graduating) and Devo drummer Alan Myers.

At Firestone, Carney was an outcast who was often bullied. Tall and skinny, he eventually topped out at six-foot-four. Later, he embraced his outsider status and even confronted his bullies. A friend of his at Firestone recalled: "I thought of him as a cool kid. I looked up to him and thought, 'Pat's cool.' He used to run with a group of tightknit friends."

Carney later admitted: "I really enjoyed high school. I never played a sport, wasn't in any clubs. Never did anything extracurricular, didn't get good grades, but I loved the social aspect of it. And music was my thing. It was my salvation in high school, really. I was never the best musician out of my friend group, but I always played and I had a passion for being in a band. I'd form bands and when those broke up, I'd look for other people to make a band with." According to one of his classmates, Carney was "always a musician, always in bands, always knew what deep-cut music was out. He was very knowledgeable."

During this period, Carney and some of his musician friends worked in the kitchen of a restaurant in suburban Akron, Gasoline Alley, which was co-owned by Al Kerkian, who had previously operated the blues club, Sarah's.

During the summer before his senior year of high school, 17-year-old Carney formed the band, Christopher Whispers, with classmates Gabe Schray and Steve Caynon and 22-year-old Jermaine Blair, who worked at a record store. The group practiced in the basement of Blair's home near the University of Akron.

Although most of the members were into punk rock, the group was decidedly a mainstream/alternative rock band. Carney recalled: "We were listening to Yo La Tengo, and Galaxie 500, the Feelies, stuff like that, and that was influencing the music we were making." In the group, Carney sang lead on a few songs and played the bass guitar but not drums. Still in high school, he performed with the band a few times at a restaurant in Kent, Euro Gyro, which often hosted indie-rock bands. The venue charged no admission and did not pay the acts. During this period, Carney resembled a young Buddy Holly and wore a bolo tie onstage. One of Carney's high school classmates recalled: "He definitely had a distinct look

Euro Gyro in downtown Kent.

and a distinct style, where it was different from everyone else. So he kind of dressed and looked kind of hip and cool before he was truly a rock star. He definitely had style, way more than Dan. Even though you would think that Dan had more talent in the group, Pat had way more style."

Gabe Schray, the group's drummer recalled: "Pat must of booked these two [Euro] Gyro shows. Even back then he was good at talking, networking. Pat was always precocious and ambitious. He was the first one of us to have a job on his own, which was at the Mustard Seed Market when he was like fifteen.... He was the one saving up to buy the equipment that I still can't afford, and he was always the real go-getter and wanting to do things on his own. So then later he was the one going out and getting the shows." The group also made a series of recordings on a four-track in Carney's basement.

Christopher Whispers would play just three shows before disbanding in 1998. As Schray recalled: "First Jermaine [Blair] disappeared, and we couldn't get ahold of him anymore. And then we got into this sort of high school argument with Pat, and he really wasn't talking with us. I remember Steve and I being really worried that we wouldn't have the master tapes of the Christopher Whispers recordings. And I think I talked Pat's dad into letting us go down into the basement to get something, and when we went down there, we stole the master tapes." Soon after, Carney began heading to Cleveland, where he became a part of the music scene at the indie venue, Speak In Tongues.

Later, Carney was also a member of two other bands, one of which – Example Figure Three – also included Steve Caynon. The rift between Blair and Carney eventually healed, and a few years later, when the Black Keys toured to promote their second album, the duo hired Blair's band, Intelligent Knives, as the opening act.

After high school, Carney left Akron to study photography at the Art Institute of Pittsburgh, which he later described as a "draw the turtle" type of school. He stated: "I was getting straight A's, so I knew something was wrong, because I had a 2.0 [grade point average] in high school. So that's why I left. It felt like a joke." Returning to his hometown, Carney enrolled at the University of Akron.

During this period, Carney continued to explore the local music scene and became a fan of the Akron/Kent indie-rock band, Party of Helicopters. He became good friends with the band's lead singer, Kent native Jamie Stillman, and the two men would regularly attend local rock shows. Several years later, Stillman was hired as the Black Keys' first touring manager. He knew the ins-and-outs of touring around the region in a van, something his band had done multiple times.

Later, Stillman became far better known as the founder of the Akron-based guitar pedal manufacturer, EarthQuaker Devices.

In July 2000, Carney and his future wife, Denise Grollmus, formed a band called Churchbuilder. Featuring Erin Carracher on lead vocals, the group built a small following in the city of Oberlin, where Grollmus attended the local college.

The group also played the indie-rock circuit in Northeastern Ohio at popular venues such as the Grog Shop and, as the opening act for Jonathan Richman and the Modern Lovers, the Beachland Ballroom. Churchbuilder's first Akron gig took place at a downtown venue, the Lime Spider. Signing with a small New York label, Shelflife Records, Churchbuilder recorded a full-length album, *Patty Darling*, and an EP, *Microdancer*. One of the group's fans, who saw the band perform several times, recalled: "If you listen to Churchbuilder's album, you would be shocked by the type of music Pat was making at the time. The stripped-down, gut-bucket blues of the Black Keys was the exact opposite of what Churchbuilder was about – an alternative, indie, pop kind of group."

▶ CHAPTER 3
DANIEL AUERBACH

Daniel Quine Auerbach was born on May 14, 1979, in Athens, Ohio. A vibrant college town that's home to Ohio University (not to be confused with the Ohio State University in Columbus), Athens is situated on the edge of Appalachia. When Dan was eight, he moved with his family to Akron.

On Dan's father's side, the Auerbach family descended from Polish-Jewish ancestry. His paternal grandmother was able to escape Nazi Germany shortly before the country's borders were closed. He recalled: "Her entire family was murdered. Mom, dad, elder brothers, everyone. She made it to England and learned to speak English. She met my grandpa, who was in the army, and they moved to New Jersey, and eventually reunited with my great-uncle [who survived his confinement in a concentration camp]. All those stories were a big part of my growing up. You realize how lucky we are. It certainly makes you work harder."

Auerbach's mother, a former piano teacher, came from a

family of musicians. At a young age, Dan was taught how to play guitar by his cousins. He soon began participating in family jam sessions: "Ever since I was a kid, family reunions, they'd play and sing together in a circle, do two- and three-part harmonies – playing old spiritual songs, bluegrass songs, blues songs, folk songs, a lot of Stanley Brothers tunes, a lot of Bill Monroe songs, which are basically blues songs sung by white people." During this period, Dan often accompanied his parents to watch his uncles perform around Akron.

However, Auerbach's mother – who had far different musical tastes – did not join the rest of the family during their frequent musical affairs. He recalled that his mother "was like the outcast in her family because she was into classical music, so she would play piano solo. She'd always be playing... stuff around the house."

While Auerbach's mother was employed as a French teacher, his father had a less traditional occupation. Dan explained: "My dad was an antique dealer and kind of a junk collector, so we would go out all the time into the country, searching small shops or talking to some old picker about some crazy thing he just found. It felt the same looking for these blues musicians, not knowing who you would find. It was like the magic of the hunt. It was awesome." With an aging population, Northeastern Ohio was a picker's paradise as entire estates were frequently sold at auctions and tag sales.

However, the Auerbachs had another means of acquiring treasures and collectibles. Dan recalled: "My dad did antique shows. He'd go to these big fairs in New York and Nashville a couple of times a year and I would go with him. If we set off [from Akron] on trash day, if there was something interesting poking out of the trash, no matter if all my classmates were walking by, he'd stop the van and either make me get out and look at it, or he did. Then we'd drive to NYC and I'd watch Ralph Lauren or one of the Beastie Boys buy something from him that I saw pulled out of the... trash! That was really good for me. It made me realize early on that you can get out of Akron and you can be connected to all these things." With the Auerbachs accumulating a horde of antiques, the home was often packed with merchandise, from furniture to artwork. Open space was sometimes at a premium.

Auerbach's father was also a serious music aficionado who had amassed an extensive record collection – including blues, Motown, Beatles, classic rock and blues-inspired rock like the Allman Brothers as well as some traditional Jewish music. In his youth, Dan was encouraged to listen to the collection and was taught how to properly handle and care for vinyl records. With music blaring throughout the Auerbach household, Dan recalled: "Nobody listens to music louder than my dad does." The elder Auerbach also played loud music when driving around town. Dan recalled: "He'd blast out the Stones and the Allman Brothers in the car... Yeah, and scare my friends. They'd be like, 'I've never heard music that loud before.'"

▶ CHAPTER 4
DAN GETS THE BLUES

At age 12, Dan Auerbach's mother took him to Blossom Music Center for his first concert. Sitting in the lawn area, Auerbach could barely see Whitney Houston on the distant stage. That same year, his father took him to see the Grateful Dead at the since-demolished Richfield Coliseum. Auerbach later recalled: "It was eye opening, wild. Everything was unexpected.... There were 20,000 people in this place alone and they all looked insane and they were all dancing and this was before anyone was even onstage! Then Jerry [Garcia] comes out with his white hair and beard, like Einstein. Crazy, but fun! They didn't sound like the Dead recordings I was used to, but he was cool."

Regularly exposed to blues music at home, Auerbach developed an early taste for the African-American genre, something that was very uncommon among youth in Akron – either black or white. Auerbach recalled: "When I was teaching myself to play guitar, I was listening to the blues and that's what I was trying to play." However, when he was with his friends – who had absolutely no interest in the blues – he listened to rap and alternative rock. Auerbach recalled: "There were more people listening to hip-hop at our high school than rock 'n' roll." In fact, Auerbach's first music purchase was the single, "Mind Playing Tricks On Me" by the rap act, the Geto Boys.

Growing up in a non-traditional household, Dan admitted: "I didn't really have much to rebel against.... The only way I could really rebel would be to wear a suit and tie every day and become a lawyer or something."

*   *   *   *   *   *

Dan Auerbach was given an unusual middle name, Quine. It was his mother's maiden name. It was also the last name of his cousin, Robert Quine. A notable guitarist who was raised in Akron, Quine graduated from law school but left the field to pursue a career in music. Quine recalled: "I've been playing guitar seriously since 1958. I was always obsessed with music and I had my first band by 1961. We did instrumental covers, Link Wray, that sort of stuff.... I remember playing my father a Little Richard record and he said, 'Well that's nice son but it's trash, when you mature you'll get into jazz and classical music.' But I guess I never quite matured."

After moving to San Francisco in the late-1960s, Quine was unable to find like-minded musicians. As a fan of the Velvet Underground, he wanted to form a similar group. During this period, the Velvet Underground played a series of shows in the city, with some of the performances appearing on the album,

Live – '69. After attending more than two-dozen of the group's shows, Quine was eventually befriended by the group's frontman, Lou Reed.

Relocating to New York City in 1971, Quine initially found only occasional work as a musician. For a time, he took a job at a movie memorabilia shop alongside pioneering punk rockers, Richard Hell and Tom Verlaine. Later asked to join Hell's group, the Voidoids, Quine appeared on the seminal punk album, *The Blank Generation.* "I think Quine was the best rock and roll soloist ever. He found a way to mix art with emotion that put him ahead of everyone. It's sad that he made so few recordings. His best playing was with me, and we made fewer than three albums' worth of material.... He was a complicated, volatile, sensitive, very smart person who humbly channeled everything he was and knew into his guitar playing," observed Hell.

In 1981, Robert Quine joined Lou Reed's backing band for the album, *Blue Mask.* Reed later explained: "Quine got me playing guitar again. I quit playing guitar with bands... because I couldn't get along with the other musicians. Quine was really encouraging about my playing, saying, 'You've got to play lead.' Now, that's my kind of guy!" By 1991, Quine had attracted a new generation of fans after he provided the guitarwork on Matthew Sweet's alternative rock hit, "Girlfriend."

Meanwhile, Auerbach's uncle Jim was his first musical mentor. Auerbach recalled: "He taught me how to play my first song on guitar. He was helping me out when I was 15 years old, showing me chords and stuff." Soon after, Auerbach was given an electric guitar, a rare and expensive instrument which he traded for a very cheap Japanese knockoff – a worn '60s Teisco/Kawai. He later recalled: "My mom got me a Stratocaster, but I was trying to be like Hound Dog Taylor, so I took it to [a music store] in Cleveland, and traded it. A two-thousand-dollar guitar, for this. I was clueless." Auerbach added: "The guy at the store was like, 'Yeah, sounds like a great deal to me. You might even be coming out ahead.'"

Around this time, Auerbach had a long visit with Robert Quine in Akron. Auerbach recalled: "He lived in NYC and my parents basically made him sit down with me and play guitar. His mom's name is Rosalie – and Rosalie said, 'Bobby, he's gonna be here at noon. You have to sit down with him' ... So I arrived and I had my Junior Kimbrough record and my Teisco Del Ray guitars and he was overjoyed. We hung out for hours. He was telling me all about how he was so excited I was into the stuff he was into. He didn't get along with my family, as he's not the nicest guy to people who aren't interested in the exact same things as him. But we connected." Quine also instructed Auerbach to look him up if he ever came to New York. Sadly, the Black Keys wouldn't make it to the city until 2004, a few months after Quine had died.

*   *   *   *   *   *

While still at Firestone High School, Dan Auerbach became a serious student of pioneering Delta blues players such as Robert Johnson and Son House. Auerbach was particularly drawn to a distinct sub-genre called North Mississippi hill country blues, which was epitomized by guitarists Junior Kimbrough, Big Joe Williams and R.L. Burnside. The genre

The new Firestone High School in Akron.

was originated by self-taught guitarist Fred McDowell, who was discovered in 1959 by notable musicologist, Alan Lomax.

Auerbach recalled: "The first time I heard the North Mississippi sound was in Alan Lomax's field recordings of Fred McDowell's Arhoolie label recordings. I fell in love with that stuff, and Fred's 'Write Me A Few Of Your Lines' became a favorite song. With this stuff, some people get it, some people don't." In 1971, 67-year-old McDowell would perform at a nightclub in Kent as a duo with Robert Kidney of the Numbers Band. That same year, the Rolling Stones included a rendition of McDowell's "You Got To" on the album, *Sticky Fingers*.

However, Auerbach was not a fan of all blues styles: "I didn't even like Chicago blues, because it sounded too clean. I was obsessed with early, electric Memphis blues. Those guys were totally untrained, playing with their fingers. And all the amps were small and turned up too loud. Or just broken."

Mostly self-taught on guitar, Auerbach recalled: "I loved the sounds all the old blues guys were making so I just copied them. It was a case of repetition reaping rewards: I would listen to the record, try to play it, get it wrong, and listen to it again. Eventually I understood what it was they were doing." Auerbach also studied the live performances of his blues influences: "I used to get videos from the library – blues and bluegrass guys – and just watch how they did it. Watch their hands, pause it, rewind, replay, over and over again for hours. I remember getting [Les Blank's 1967 documentary film] *The Blues Accordin' To Lightnin' Hopkins*, and watching it was just humongous for me."

Auerbach insisted: "If you watch them enough times, and then listen to the records, you can work it out. At first I didn't know the names of the chords or the techniques that they were using – that came later. But it was so cool to manage to make a noise that sounded good, even if I couldn't play the song that it was a part of." Later, Auerbach received occasional lessons from a local blues guitarist, Mike Lenz.

CHAPTER 5

THE BLUES IN MISSISSIPPI

In 1996, 17-year-old Dan Auerbach and his father took a road trip to the home of the blues in the northern region of Mississippi. Along the way, they stopped in Memphis to watch a sermon by former soul music star, the Rev. Al Green.

Traveling through the Delta region, Auerbach observed: "It reminded me of southern Ohio, where I was born." Reaching their destination, the Auerbachs entered a ramshackle juke joint – owned by guitarist Junior Kimbrough – near the small town of Holly Springs. Auerbach recalled: "Outside, the joint looked as if it was about to cave in, very haphazard with a lot of plywood. But it was incredible inside. The walls were painted different colors and there was glitter paint. There were portraits lining the walls of great black leaders.... There was a tiny little counter in the back where they sold beer and there was no stage, just a little spot where the musicians played. At a certain time, people just started to show up either by car and on horseback.... That was the first time I ever saw a black cowboy. I didn't even know they existed. The whole thing was amazing and I suddenly realized that I was in a totally different universe. The people were very welcoming and the music was very special."

However, Junior Kimbrough was in a hospital at the time. Auerbach recalled: "We met his son Kinny, who plays drums on all the records. Kinny let us know Junior was really sick and hadn't played in months. But he said if we could lend him some money to get his brother David out of jail, he could bring him here. 'He plays daddy's songs' is what he said." After paying the $24 bail, Auerbach recalled: "It was amazing. I got to hear all those songs, and it was at Junior's juke joint. It wasn't Junior but it was his family. Everyone was having a good time. I did see a gun pulled, but it never got fired."

Auerbach was deeply inspired by the experience. *The New York Times* reported: "Auerbach, needing to see more, took a second trip down to Greenville shortly thereafter. On that second trip, Auerbach slept on the floor of [blues guitarist] T-Model Ford's double-wide trailer. He was still a teenager when T-Model Ford invited him to join him onstage, first at a house party and then at a juke joint. It was a crash course – not just in how to play the music but also in how to play to a crowd, how to keep people excited, invested in what was happening both on the stage and [among] themselves." Auerbach remembered: "It was just like in the middle of a field. Just absolutely in the middle of nowhere in a cinder-block building. I played all night there."

Unfortunately, Auerbach never got to see Junior Kimbrough, who would pass away the following year: "I drove down to

The Kimbrough Brothers: David Jr., Kinney and Robert, left to right, at the Clarksdale Juke Joint Festival.

Mississippi three times to see him but he was sick each time.... I'm glad I got to go before [his juke joint] burned down." The building was reduced to ashes in 2000.

Meanwhile, at Firestone High School, Auerbach wasn't a standout student. He had long hair and was the captain of the soccer team. Pat Carney, who was one grade behind Auerbach, recalled that his future musical partner "hung out with more of a jock kind of crowd and I hung out with more of a... smart-ass group. Mostly his friends and my friends didn't get along." Auerbach recalled: "We were in different grades. So, you know how when you're in different grades it's like being in a whole different universe? So, we didn't really have the same friends or anything like that. But we knew each other, we rode the same bus. Stuff like that." According to one of Auerbach's classmates, he wasn't known in high school for his musical skills: "Dan was like a jock in high school... not too much of a musician. I'm sure he was playing, but not like in bands like Pat was."

Although Auerbach and Carney had little in common at the time, Auerbach later revealed that the two teens did share one thing: "We both had the same middle school bully." At Firestone, Auerbach spent a great deal of time in detention, where he secretly listened to a portable cassette player.

▶ CHAPTER 6
THE BARNBURNERS

After graduating from high school, Dan Auerbach attended Mount Union College in Alliance, a forty-minute drive from Akron. He recalled: "Worst decision of my life – there wasn't even a record shop." He subsequently transferred to the University of Akron, which at the time had an enrollment of 25,000 students. The mid-sized school was founded in 1870 as Buchtel College. The school's mascot, Zippy the Kangaroo, was inspired by the school's nickname, the Zips. Quickly losing interest in his schoolwork, Auerbach began skipping classes to hone his guitar skills.

He took a job as a clerk at an Akron record store, Quonset Hut: "I was exposed to things there that I never would have heard otherwise. I remember this Frank Black and the Catholic album that I loved. We also sold a lot of Deadhead merchandise." (Pat Carney worked at a different Quonset Hut location on the other side of town.) Auerbach also spent a summer as a parking lot attendant at Blossom Music Center, a large outdoor venue that he would one day headline. Auerbach's job did not include the privilege of seeing the concerts: "But I did hear the music, and it was really cool being out in the woods, seeing thousands of people flooding into the show."

In 1999, Auerbach performed on an Akron stage for the very first time. He recalled: "The first time I ever played in front of a crowd was on a Tuesday night at the Northside Lounge in Akron.... I had been taking guitar lessons from this guy and he was playing there. He knew I knew a bunch of old songs so he invited me to come up and play. I got on stage and my ears shut off, I was sweating like crazy, I was completely terrified. It took me ten minutes to tune up." The Northside Lounge – now the site of Jilly's Music Room – was located about fifty-feet from where Chrissie Hynde would later open a vegetarian restaurant.

Losing his stage fright, Auerbach would perform at the venue several times over the next year. He also occasionally played at Mugs in Kent and the Mustard Seed Market in Montrose – where his future bandmate Pat Carney had previously worked in the kitchen.

Meanwhile, Auerbach wanted to quit school: "My dad told me that if I dropped out, I'd have to start playing gigs and making a living out of it. So I started doing three, four, five nights a week at bars all around Akron. Sometimes it would just be me sitting on a chair, playing a guitar for three hours. I was, like, 18. The shows could be fun as hell or super depressing." He added: "Whatever the club needed I would provide. If they just needed a solo act, I would do that. If they wanted a two-piece, I would do that. If they wanted a full band, I had a couple of drummers I would call. And honestly, nothing is better practice than playing in front of people." However, his performances weren't always well-received: "People weren't even listening at some places, so I'd just play an N.W.A. song."

Auerbach also performed at a busy, open-air bus shelter on South Main Street in downtown Akron, which was situated in front of a former department store. He recalled: "[My father was] pushing me to be the new Hound Dog Taylor. He would make me go on Main Street and play for change at the bus stop, because I didn't have a job." However, he later revealed: "I was actually making pretty good money!"

Meanwhile, local bandleader Patrick Sweany caught a performance by Auerbach at the bus shelter. Sweany recalled: "[Auerbach] was great, he could play before he knew the names of the strings. But he could flat out play, man. He didn't run out of ideas and he started telling me about the garage rock he was into, the Greenhornes and stuff. I was pretty much on my blues island; anything that wasn't made by dead black people, I didn't like... His dad [Chuck] brought him to gigs and we got to know each other and he joined the band." For the next two-years, Auerbach played in the Patrick Sweany Band at a Monday night residency in downtown Kent.

Later, Auerbach fronted his own band, the Barnburners, which played a mixture of rockabilly and electric blues. Clean-shaven at the time, Auerbach provided the lead vocals and played guitar. He was joined in the trio by Jason Edwards on drums and Kip Amore (a.k.a. Johnny Belvedere) on standup bass. In 2001, the group released *The Rawboogie EP*, which was highlighted by the Junior Kimbrough classic, "Meet Me In The City." For more than a year, the band enjoyed a Thursday night residency at the Northside in downtown Akron. On occasion, Auerbach's uncle, Tim Quine, joined the group on blues harp.

▶ CHAPTER 7
DAN & PAT REUNITE

After briefly enrolling at separate out-of-town colleges, Dan Auerbach and Pat Carney reunited while attending the University of Akron. Soon after, the two young men worked for the same landscaping company and mowed lawns around the city. However, Auerbach and Carney disagree on how they first connected as musicians.

Auerbach claims he first got together with Carney as a result of a common friend who played the harmonica: "His name was Steve and he was into blues music and so was I – so that's how we knew each other. He knew Pat, and one day he was like, 'Let's go over there – he's got a drum kit.' We went over there and played stupid music really loud. Pat played drums really similar to the way he does now. You know what I mean. Like unschooled hip-hop beats, or whatever they are. And I was playing open-tunings – things like Fred McDowell that I was just learning – in a loud distorted way. Our friend was playing harmonica through my amp, and it was fun. We decided to get together and keep playing, but basically Steve stopped coming and then it was me and Pat. At a certain point we broke out the four-track [mixing board], and then, before you knew it, I'd be down in his parents' basement recording. Or he'd be at my parents' house, and we'd set up the drum kit, and then hang mikes from the shower curtain."

Carney offered his own recollection: "Me and Dan had jammed in high school, but it was infrequent. We ran into each other in a record store and hadn't jammed in a year or so." During this period, Carney had lost a pair of jobs – as a telemarketer and a worker at the Highland Square Theater, and was at a low point in his life.

Carney added: "I had a summer off, and I was about to go to college at the University of Akron for my third year, not knowing what... I wanted to do. I just played with this [Korg digital 12-track] recorder and I got pretty good with it. Dan was like, 'Do you want to record my band?' I said, 'Of course, man! Come over to my house.' He showed up and we waited on my front porch. It was a late, hot, summer day. The other guys never showed up. Dan was like, 'Shit, why don't you play the drums?' I was a guitar player; I could barely play the drums. The only time I'd ever played the drums was when I played with Dan years earlier."

Suddenly, Carney was forced to switch to an instrument he had yet to master: "I didn't know how to play the drums, I truly didn't. I had bought a drum set when I was 15, but it was for other people to come to my house to play." Auerbach described the instant musical bond between the two men: "It was immediate, we could immediately make something.... We never really hung out, we just were really good at making music

44

together. But we did become friends, and we became people who really genuinely love and care for each other." However, Carney later admitted, "If it hadn't been for music, we probably wouldn't be friends."

Auerbach and Carney never intended to be a two-man musical outfit. After a few jam sessions – which featured a keyboardist and harmonica player – the outfit was pared down to a duo. Auerbach recalled, "We auditioned a couple people when we started, and every time we would add that other person, we would sound smaller and shittier. We always sounded more dynamic and exciting when there was just two of us."

▶ CHAPTER 8
THE KEYS HOOK UP

The Black Keys formed in July 2001 with little fanfare. Auerbach recalled: "There's something about Akron. It's an old factory town. So people are blue-collar. They've got their 'factory mentality.' Pat and I, as soon as we decided that the Black Keys was going to be a band, we worked every single day. It was like clockwork." The duo spent their days practicing, usually quitting at 4PM. While Carney went to work at the Gasoline Alley restaurant, Auerbach would join his *other* band for a nightclub gig.

Feeling "miserable and directionless," Carney soon followed Auerbach's lead and dropped out of the University of Akron. He recalled his family's reaction: "When I told my dad and grandfather that I was going to drop out of school, my dad was against it, but my grandfather – who had a PhD in chemical engineering – was surprisingly supportive. He said, 'Give it two years and if it doesn't work out you can go back to school.'"

Carney insisted: "There was no plan B. I guess I would have started a landscaping company or something. But I don't know what I would have done. I think one of the things that really helped Dan and I was we got rid of our life preservers early on. We both dropped out of school together and made basically an unspoken pact to make this thing work."

The duo's name was inspired by Alfred McMoore, a local artist who was schizophrenic. Carney explained: "A black key [on a piano] sounds dissonant to him. It's a foul sound. He'd call you a black key if you wouldn't do what he wanted. Literally the only two households on the planet that would understand that name was Dan's and mine."

Auerbach recalled: "[McMoore] lived in a group home and would generally wear at least four three-piece suits, all at the same time, one on top of the other, layered. My dad... would try to help him out, to keep him in art supplies and things, so he was around the house a lot when I was growing up."

Auerbach and Carney spent several weeks practicing in the basement of a house Carney was renting with friends, which wasn't in the best part of town. Carney revealed: "I basically lived in a crack house. Well, it wasn't a crack house, but all the houses next door were. It was 'hood. It was a really dangerous neighborhood." He also recalled: "I remember having to pick up dead rats in the kitchen. With a *Cleveland Scene* magazine, we'd just scoop them up, roll them up in the magazine. Then we'd just go down into the basement and continue to practice."

The basement's walls were constructed of rectangular gray blocks. The room was illuminated by one small window and a bare lightbulb hanging from the ceiling. Behind them on the wall was a black velvet painting of a silver unicorn and a bulky,

Pat Carney's house in Akron where the Black Keys recorded their first two albums.

natural gas meter. Carney later gave the studio two different names – Studio 45 and Synch Etiquette Analog Sound.

The Black Keys finally recorded a demo in August 2001. During the sessions, they received some input from Ralph Carney, Pat's uncle. The completed demo was mailed to fifteen different labels. The package included a short handwritten biography of the Black Keys, which falsely stated they regularly performed around the Cleveland area. Nevertheless, before playing a single time in public, the two men attracted the attention of Alive Records, a small independent label in Burbank, California, operated by noted rock journalist, Greg Shaw. Carney later admitted: "We were shocked when we got a record deal." However, instead of offering royalty payments, the label promised to give the two men 50 vinyl LPs and 200 CDs of their album.

▶ CHAPTER 9
THE BIG COME UP

In February 2002, the Black Keys recorded their first album, with Pat Carney listed as the producer. He later explained: "I mean, I would say technically I didn't produce [the album]. I think at the time we didn't really know what the terminology was. We didn't even know what producing was until we worked with a producer. We realized that we'd been producing ourselves all along."

For the project, the duo employed a new mixing board that Carney had purchased on credit. Carney recalled: "My dad was so stressed out that I'd gone into $1,000 of debt, but we just worked every day. Dan would come over to the house at 10:30AM and start yelling outside or honk his horn to wake me up because we didn't have cell phones."

For the album, the Black Keys were striving for a mid-fidelity sound, as opposed to a completely raw, low-fidelity approach. They used $18 Chinese-made microphones from Radio Shack, which were hung from the basement's water pipes. On one occasion, they placed a mic inside a washing machine as an experiment. Eventually, the mics were plugged into a Maestro fuzz pedal to get the desired sound. Auerbach played a vintage, gold-tone '60s Harmony Stratotone guitar. During the sessions, the furnace was turned off in order to avoid the sound of burning natural gas.

The 13-song project consisted mostly of originals plus a few covers of blues classics by R.L. Burnside and Junior Kimbrough. Also included was a remake of the psychedelic Beatles track, "She Said, She Said," which featured Gabe Fulvimar on a Moog bass. Auerbach and Carney offered to hire Fulvimar as a full-time member, but he was not interested in joining the outfit.

The debut Black Keys album, *The Big Come Up*, was released on Auerbach's 23rd birthday in May 2002. The album was completed before the duo had ever played a live date. The first single, "Leavin' Trunk," was a straightforward rendition of the traditional blues/folk standard. Amazingly, the album was reviewed by *Rolling Stone*, which gave it four stars. Another music critic wrote: "Despite their youth, you'd swear Dan Auerbach and Pat Carney were ancient, toothless and wizened blues wizards by the ragged depth of their groovy sound." As a result of the unexpected exposure, the album sold 500 copies in the first month, surprising the duo's label. Eventually, it would go on to sell more than 250,000 copies.

In the meantime, both members of the Black Keys were still working a number of side jobs in order to pay their bills. Carney was washing dishes in the evenings. Auerbach recalled: "I remember the day we got the review we still had to go out and mow lawns. But it was great. It was pretty surreal." In the

The Beachland Ballroom on the east side of Cleveland.

interim period, Auerbach was still earning a steady income as a member of the Barnburners.

The Black Keys performed in public for the first time in

March 2002 at the Beachland Ballroom on the east side of Cleveland. There were four acts on the bill that night. The popular venue previously housed the Croatian Liberty Home.

Although the Black Keys were told their set should run at least thirty-minutes, there was a problem. Auerbach remembered: "We're like, 'No problem, we got that.' We played everything twice as fast. Totally blacked out. We did like 10 songs or something in 20 minutes." Consequently, they ran out of songs to play. After the frenetic set, an out-of-breath Auerbach ran backstage and reflected on his performance. Carney, meanwhile, admitted: "I thought I was going to puke the whole time."

The duo performed its first Akron show at the Lime Spider. Basone recalled: "They didn't have that garage rock sound, they had more of a blues rock [sound]. I'm very surprised at how quickly they took off." He also recalled: "Being a drummer and being in a band with my brother, who's a bass player, I've always had that foundation of the rhythm section, so I really wasn't into the low-fi thing at the time. So hearing them for the first time, I was like, 'It needs bass, I don't get it.'"

The Black Keys soon went on the road for a series of grueling tours. Carney and Auerbach had devised a simple business plan – acquire a minivan and play for any club that would hire them. However, a serious mishap nearly derailed the duo later in the year. Auerbach recalled: "I remember Pat's drum kit exploding at one of our very first gigs, and [my father] gave us money to go buy nice drum hardware." A music critic would later note that Carney "pounds the drums harder than anyone you've ever seen, like King Kong throwing a tantrum."

Carney remembered the moment the duo had finally

The Lime Spider, right, on South Main Street in Akron.

achieved some success: "At first, we had to tour in my minivan playing little music halls to literally nobody. Literally, nobody. The first couple shows we played to, like, 10 people. Then we got to Seattle and 150 people came out to see us. That was huge; that was a high point. We were totally confused but totally giddy that so many people showed up. It made us want to keep going, even during the summer, in a van without air conditioning."

Auerbach was also stunned: "In Seattle, people were singing along to our songs. They knew the words. That was really surreal."

However, the duo quickly fell back to Earth. Auerbach recalled: "We played the next night at the Satyricon in Portland, Oregon, and no one showed up, maybe three people, and they'd just done local clown wrestling the night before, where they threw cake on each other as the grand finale, and the stage was carpet, so the carpet was gooey, filled with cake. It was so gross."

Meanwhile, the press began comparing the Black Keys to a blues-rock duo from nearby Detroit – the White Stripes. A *Rolling Stone* reviewer called the Black Keys "a killer, bluesy Midwest two-piece who aren't the White Stripes." Another critic wrote: "The Black Keys aren't all that cute; they don't dress in matching outfits, and they aren't likely to be the darlings of MTV any time soon. But that doesn't mean they can't be spoken of in the same breath as the White Stripes."

Auerbach explained: "When we started out, we had no idea who the White Stripes were. We never would have named ourselves the Black Keys if we *had* known about them. We don't pay much attention to the White Stripes comparison thing – it's kind of pointless, I mean, there are similarities, but they are certainly more pop-oriented than we are." One rock critic pointed out the biggest difference between the two acts: "You won't find the White Stripes in the blues section of your favorite indie record store."

▶ CHAPTER 10
KEYS TO SUCCESS

Going on the road for extended tours, the Black Keys paid their dues as they solidified their sound and built a loyal fanbase. Carney revealed: "We like challenges. When we first decided to be a band, the goal was for us each to make about $150 a week, and we were able to do that within four months of our first show in March 2002. We've supported ourselves ever since."

Auerbach recalled: "We used to drive nine hours to get to a gig, get paid 30 dollars and then, because we couldn't afford to stay in town, drive two hours to somewhere cheap outside of the city. I mean, every day. We weren't able to party or have a drink after a show really until 2008... We had to drive to the Motel 6. Pat was always able to drive late at night. No problem. I think we were aware that being in a band was going to be hard work, but we didn't know how much hard work." The duo was occasionally joined on the road by Carney's brother, Mike.

In May, the Black Keys were the subject of a feature story

for the first time when Peter Relic interviewed the duo for the now-defunct Cleveland arts magazine, *The Free Times*. (Later, Relic briefly worked as the duo's tour manager.) On July 21, the Black Keys were mentioned for the first time in their hometown paper, *The Akron Beacon Journal*, in a listing for an upcoming show at the Cleveland Agora. The duo was one of the four scheduled opening acts at a concert headlined by local punk-metal band, Disengage.

Around Akron, there was a growing buzz surrounding the duo. In October, *The Akron Beacon Journal* published its first article about the Black Keys with the headline, "Akron Duo Seems on Verge of the Big Time." In the piece, a clearly apprehensive Carney admitted: "I'm nervous about messing up (on stage), I'm nervous about the whole thing. I just want the whole situation to kind of end." (Years later, Carney would reveal: "I actually had anxiety issues for the first year and half when it started. I couldn't make sense of it. It was very surreal.")

Sensing that the duo was about to break out, a number of major labels began showing interest. But instead of traveling to Los Angeles or New York, the two members of the Black Keys made the label representatives come to Akron. Over the next few months, the two musicians were wined and dined at various restaurants around the city.

Sire Records was one of the labels that courted the Black Keys. The company's president, Seymour Stein – who had previously signed the Pretenders – came to a Black Keys show at the Beachland Ballroom in Cleveland and spoke with the duo. Carney later explained: "For two middle-class kids from Akron, the idea of a major label giving us $100,000 was very tempting – we could have bought houses and recorded in a really nice studio. But if we would have done that we wouldn't be around right now. We would have been dropped on our third or fourth album and we would never have been touched again by another major label."

While touring through the South, the Black Keys made a visit to the headquarters of Fat Possum Records, a label that specialized in Delta blues. Auerbach and Carney met with the company's owners – Matthew Johnson and Bruce Watson – and discussed their shared love of the blues. Johnson later recalled: "They looked so young, young visitors to a bad planet. Bruce was able to find them a show at the Long Shot in Oxford. I think one of the old cobwebbed deer heads fell on Dan. I remember the owner walking downstairs from his apartment into the bar and saying something like: 'They kinda suck. A bass player would help a lot.'"

Carney recalled: "Within two hours, they're negotiating if we would take a 1982 Mercedes with bullet holes in it as part of our record contract. Because they were trying to get the money down. They're like, 'How about maybe five grand and that car?'"

After coming to an agreement, the Black Keys became the youngest act at the Mississippi-based record company. Carney recalled: "We were talking to some bigger labels who were dragging their feet. And Fat Possum had been talking to us on the phone pretty much every day for five months." However, Carney added: "We were nervous to sign with Fat Possum. They are considered a blues label, so we knew it would be harder to resist being labeled as a blues band. But the guys at Fat Possum are such sweet dudes that we figured they would help us figure out a way to work around that." Auerbach also noted: "It's funny because we originally sent our [original] demo to Fat Possum and they totally ignored it."

The members of the Black Keys would later realize that signing with a smaller label was the right thing to do at that stage of their career. Carney would later admit that Matthew Johnson "taught us a lot about music – about the kind of hustle it takes to kind of be a band that we weren't really aware of at the time."

The Black Keys played a hometown show on October 26 at the Lime Spider. Admission was $5. That same month, Akron radio station, WAPS, began playing the duo's track, "I'll Be Your Man." And in December, the Black Keys finally headlined a show at the Beachland Ballroom.

▶ CHAPTER 11
THICKFREAKNESS

In late-2002, the Black Keys recorded some tracks at a San Francisco studio. They were invited to the city by producer Jeff Saltzman, who paid for the studio time and offered to manage the duo. However, both Auerbach and Carney were unhappy with the sessions, which were more rock-oriented than their debut album. These recordings were never released. (Saltzman would later have success with the popular alternative-rock band, the Killers.)

Returning to Akron, the Black Keys realized that their basement studio was far more suited to recording blues music. Carney explained: "We wanted this thing to sound better than a home recording but still have a rough quality.... We've done stuff in fancy studios [and] that sounds like garbage to us."

The duo's second album, *Thickfreakness*, was recorded during just one 14-hour session in December 2002, using a vintage 8-track Tascam mixer. The project featured two cover songs – Richard Berry's "Have Love, Will Travel" and Junior Kimbrough's "Everywhere I Go."

*   *   *   *   *   *

In 2003, the Black Keys endured a hectic but productive year. Both members of the duo were determined to succeed. Auerbach insisted: "We always thought of this like a business. We worked our asses off on it. But by the time the Black Keys broke, we were just on the road so much. You're waking up every day and it's the same exact thing. Same backstage room, routine, questions, answers, same outfit. It can be maddening if you let it. You have to learn to turn your brain off. But we learned to make it work." Meanwhile, both members of the duo often wore clothing with Akron references, and Dan Auerbach would begin shows with his soon-to-be signature greeting, "We're the Black Keys from Akron." Likewise, Carney insisted, "Everywhere we go, we let people know where we're from."

In January, the Black Keys played a series of dates as the opening act for the alternative-rock act, Sleater-Kinney. At one of the Black Keys' early shows, a reviewer wrote: "The Black Keys got the crowd hopping with a raunchy electric-boogie sound that pays homage to blues forebears like Junior Kimbrough." That same month, the duo had a chance meeting with alternative rocker Beck at a *Saturday Night Live* after-party in New York City. At a swanky nightclub, Pat Carney handed Beck a pre-release copy of their second album. A few months later, the Black Keys were invited to open some dates for the hit singer-songwriter.

In March, the Black Keys drove 22-hours in their overworked minivan to the annual South by Southwest music festival in Austin, Texas, which showcased more than 1,000 bands. They were accompanied by a reporter from their hometown newspaper. Additionally, Ralph Carney flew in from San Francisco to join the band onstage for a few songs at each of their three performances. After playing at Stubb's and Antone's, they finished with a show at a private party sponsored by Levi's. Afterward, Carney stated: "We feel lucky. At least we played well and the crowd was receptive. There are a lot of bands here, all trying to get noticed."

One reviewer said of the duo: "Another band building momentum at South by Southwest was the Black Keys, who may end up being one of the year's breakout stars.... Singer-guitarist Dan Auerbach wails like a second coming of Jimi Hendrix and Otis Redding and drummer Patrick Carney combines powerful rock pounding with the occasional slick hip-hop beat to create something completely new that still sounds comfortably familiar."

However, Auerbach stated at the time: "We're trying not to let the hype affect us. Good press is nice. But it doesn't pay the bills."

Meanwhile, the April release of *Thickfreakness* was celebrated with CD release parties at a pair of nightclubs in Akron and Cleveland. Pat Carney and his brother, Mike, came up with the idea for the album's striking cover after spotting a container of Royal Crown hair pomade during a late-night shopping trip at a 24-hour Super K-Mart just west of Akron.

The album's first single, "Set You Free," was a crunching, psychedelic-tinged blues-rock effort that was reminiscent of Jimi Hendrix. The duo submitted a video of the track to MTV. A few months later, the cable network inadvertently aired the clip instead of a scheduled clip by the similarly named, pop-rap group, the Black Eyed Peas. Also that year, the track was included on the soundtrack album of the Jack Black film, *School Of Rock*. Astonishingly, neither Auerbach nor Carney was told about the song's inclusion. The music-themed comedy film was a surprise hit and brought a great deal of attention to the Black Keys.

Later in April, the Black Keys played their first shows in Europe – two in London and one in Paris. Carney recalled: "After this record came out it was the first time we got to tour Europe." The Black Keys' early success in the U.K. was largely due to influential British deejay John Peel, who was the first to play their music in Europe. During the brief tour, the duo also performed on Peel's BBC Radio 1 show. The duo would return to Europe a few months later for a short, sold-out tour.

In July, the Black Keys headed to the West Coast for a number of shows. While performing in Los Angeles, they experienced their first taste of rock stardom. Carney recalled: "We were getting weird phone calls, people like the producer of *Friends*, who was looking for tickets. And label reps from RCA would come backstage and tell us, 'If you ever need anything let us know.' We didn't know what that meant. I think it was just if we wanted drugs."

In August, the duo made their national television debut with an appearance on *Late Night With Conan*. For the occasion, Carney wore a Tin Huey t-shirt that he was given by a member of the Akron new wave group. Both men were noticeably hyped during their energetic performance of the track, "Thickfreakness." Carney recalled: "I remember the first time we played a late-night show. It was '03 and we played *Conan*, and I flew straight back to Akron and went to the Lime Spider and watched it on TV there, just to see the band on TV. It was exciting to have the opportunity, and we were playing where a lot of my favorite bands had played." The nightclub was packed that night with Black Keys fans, who cheered on the group.

Later that month, the duo launched a three-month tour. For the first time, both members decided to bring along their girlfriends. After playing a pair of festival shows in Europe, the Black Keys headed to Australia, where they had already established a strong fanbase.

Without the aid of a traditional promotional campaign, the Black Keys were on a quick ascent. At the end of 2003, Auerbach told a reporter: "This whole year's been shocking. We didn't expect anything like this to happen to us. We just wanted to play shows and we've played 165 of them this year." Nevertheless, Carney insisted: "We always feel like the underdogs."

▶ CHAPTER 12
RUBBER CITY BLUES

Returning to Akron, the Black Keys began planning the sessions for their next album. However, Carney's landlord sold the house where they had recorded their first two albums. With the help of Carney's mother, who worked as a real estate agent, the duo found a space they could rent on a short-term basis.

The duo's third album was recorded in a mostly unoccupied, former General Tire factory, where passenger tires were last manufactured in 1982. Paying $500 a month for a large room on the second floor of the crumbling building on the east side of Akron, the duo assembled a rudimentary recording studio, which they named Sentient Sound. The sessions began in January 2004 and were completed in early-May.

For the sessions, Auerbach and Carney used an oversized Tascam mixing board that once belonged to the 1980s Canadian rock band, Loverboy. Carney purchased the board on eBay for $550 and paid an additional $500 for the seller to personally transport it from Canada to Akron. However, with the device often malfunctioning, the recording process took longer than planned.

Carney recalled: "The rubber factory was a really disgusting place. It was actually difficult to work there. It was obviously more comfortable to be at home." Every afternoon, the pair would take a break and head to a nearby diner that was open 24-hours a day. Auerbach recalled: "I had a ham and cheese omelet every day, and Pat would have a patty melt with french fries." After the completion of the sessions, Auerbach and Carney abandoned the mixing board. It was still there a few years later when they returned.

When the Black Keys announced a show at Akron's Lime Spider in March, the concert sold out almost immediately! The club's owner, Danny Basone, recalled: "Literally within three gigs of playing here, we put the tickets on TicketWeb, which we were using, and they sold out in a minute. We called TicketWeb and asked, 'Is there something wrong, we just posted this show?'" In all, the Black Keys would perform at the Lime Spider a total of six times.

The Black Keys' self-produced album, *Rubber Factory*, was released in September. It was the duo's first album to chart on *Billboard's* sales chart, peaking at #143. The front and back of the cover featured a number of Akron landmarks, including the massive Goodyear Air Dock, a group of four Goodyear blimps, the Tangier restaurant and an establishment frequented by both members of the duo, Hamburger Station. Carney – who had just purchased his first home – stated at the time: "I think with each record, our sound has developed a little bit more, we've developed a little bit more, we've changed a little bit. As long as you continue to do that, you're fine."

Harvey Gold, formerly of Tin Huey, performing with the HiFis.

The album's first single, the upbeat blues-rocker "10 A.M. Automatic," was well received. The song's video was filmed by Harvey Gold – formerly of the pioneering Akron new wave group Tin Huey – and directed by comedian David Cross. In the clip, the Black Keys stage a performance for a group of elderly people. However, when one overexcited woman attempts to touch Auerbach, she is carried off by a pair of brawny bouncers. (The clip was later ranked the #24 best video of the decade by *Paste* magazine.)

The album's other standout tracks included "Till I Get My Way" and "Girl Is On My Mind." There were two cover songs on the album, including "Grown So Ugly," which was originally recorded by Robert Pete Williams, a bluesman who spent 12-years in prison for killing a man in a bar fight.

Going on the road to promote the album, the duo experienced some unforeseen difficulties. Carney explained: "We'd done so much overdubbing on *Rubber Factory*, it was hard for us as a two-piece to actually go out and play those songs 'cause a lot of them were just studio creations. I'd be playing a fiddle, I'd be playing acoustic guitar and we'd be just doing all sorts of weird shit on the songs." During a show in Sante Fe, New Mexico, Billy Gibbons of ZZ Top was in the audience.

In the autumn of 2004, the Black Keys toured across Europe. Traveling in a crowded van along with three grumpy roadies, Auerbach and Carney found the experience very unpleasant. As Auerbach recalled: "We hit the fan. It was really... awful. We came back [to Akron] and I didn't think I would ever go on tour again. We cancelled an upcoming tour and we basically had to regroup." Despite the overall success of the European dates, the tour ended with a $3,000 loss.

*   *   *   *   *   *

In 2005, Pat Carney teamed with local musician Jamie Stillman – formerly of the Party of Helicopters – to launch a record label, Audio Eagle, which was distributed by Fat Possum Records. The label's first release was the album, *Bloodsongs*, by Youngstown-based Gil Mantera's Party Dream. Staying loyal to his hometown, Carney stated at the time: "We aren't making a lot of money yet, but we're doing well for Akron. I don't like it when bands move to a big city to become part of a scene or because their video store has a better selection." Also that year, the Black Keys' rendition of the Junior Kimbrough blues standard, "Everywhere I Go," was ranked #87 on *Classic Rock* magazine's list of the Top-100 Blues Anthems.

The following year, Audio Eagle showcased its entire roster of acts at the Lime Spider in Akron, with Carney taking the stage on electric guitar. Anxious before the show, he said at the time: "Once we sound-check, we should be fine, but I haven't played guitar onstage since 2000."

Around this time, Auerbach constructed his own studio in Akron with the assistance of noted recording engineer, Mark Neill. The two men shared a love for vintage recording equipment. At the studio, the Black Keys recorded the tribute album, *Chulahoma: The Songs of Junior Kimbrough*. Kimbrough's son, Kinney, said of the six-song project: "Listen, it is hard to play my dad's music. I grew up playing it with the man, and I still can't get it sometimes. So they're doing all right for themselves here." This was the Black Keys' final album for Fat Possum Records.

With the expiration of their three-album deal with Fat Possum, the Black Keys were looking to sign with a larger record company. But instead of traveling to New York or Los Angeles to meet with interested labels, the duo once again instructed the companies to send their representatives to Akron. Over a three-week period, Auerbach and Carney were wined and dined by record company executives at various restaurants around the city. That same year, Auerbach's early musical influence, R.L. Burnside, passed away at the age of 78.

Meanwhile, the Black Keys began opening for top level acts like Radiohead and Pearl Jam. Carney was involved in an unfortunate squabble after one of the Pearl Jam shows: "Dan and I ended up drinking lots of beer with Eddie Vedder until 4 in the morning. It was crazy. We got into a slight argument about the Who. I'd made fun of them. I didn't realize they were Eddie Vedder's favorite band. He jumped on my back and wrestled me to the ground."

▶ CHAPTER 13
BLUES AT NONESUCH

In February 2006, the Black Keys played their largest local show – up to that point – for nearly 2,000 fans at the Agora in Cleveland. Dan Auerbach stated at the time: "I was worried that no one was going to show up." For the opening act, Auerbach hired his former bandleader, Patrick Sweany. Also that year, Auerbach co-produced an album for Sweany, *C'mon, C'mere*.

Around this time, the Black Keys began working on their next album, which was recorded over a seven-week period. Auerbach explained at the time: "We had an idea for this record. We wanted to simplify, condense and focus more, because [our previous album] *Rubber Factory* was more all over the place and this is more just a rock 'n' roll album. I think it's much more subtle the way the songs fit together."

For the project, Carney constructed a basement studio in his new home: "In Akron all basements are kinda the same. They've got concrete floors and cinder-block walls and then you've got a wood ceiling. What you end up doing is just sort of embellishing the nature of the acoustics instead of trying to hide from them." Auerbach explained why the duo preferred to record in a non-traditional setting: "We like the sound of odd rooms.... The mixing desk and computer are on top of the tool desk built by the old guy who used to live there. You can hear all of that. Lots of new records have no individuality to the sound. I wanted it to sound like a band in the basement of a house in the Midwest."

In September 2006, the Black Keys released *Magic Potion*, their first major label project. It was issued on the Warner Brothers subsidiary, Nonesuch Records. The duo signed with separate labels in Europe and Australia. Amazingly, all three of Akron's biggest rock acts – Devo, Chrissie Hynde and the Black Keys – had made their way onto the Warner Brothers roster. (Coincidentally, Warner Brothers was founded in the Northeastern Ohio city of Youngstown by four young sons of Polish immigrants.)

David Bither, the senior vice president of Nonesuch, was uneasy at first about signing the duo to the label: "I knew of the Black Keys and admired them, but never imagined them for us. A lot of labels were chasing them, it turned out.... They were outside our normal comfort zone."

More rock-oriented than their previous releases, *Magic Potion* was highlighted by the tracks, "Your Touch" and "You're The One." A *Rolling Stone* reviewer proclaimed: "Dan Auerbach plays guitar and sings like he's channeling the ghost of John Lee Hooker." However, despite having complete control over sessions, the Black Keys were not happy with the results. Carney recalled: "Our worst-selling, probably our worst album. We'd got lost, in over our heads, fallen into a rut. The record came out, and just fell off, and then came the tour, in a rented minivan, three months in the middle of the winter. Just brutal. Our career could have ended there... We both knew it. What happened next is the reason we're still around."

▶ CHAPTER 14
PRODUCER DANGER MOUSE

In 2007, the Black Keys were approached by Brian Burton – better known as Danger Mouse – of the soul duo, Gnarls Barkley. Along with CeeLo Green, Burton had scored a massive pop hit the previous year with the single, "Crazy."

Burton asked Dan Auerbach and Pat Carney to write some songs for an Ike Turner comeback album. However, after Turner's sudden death from a drug overdose in December, the project was shelved. Subsequently, the Black Keys took back the unfinished tracks for their next album. Auerbach told *Rolling Stone*, "Even when we gave the songs to Ike, they felt like Black Keys songs."

Surprisingly, the Black Keys hired Burton to produce their album. Auerbach recalled: "Brian told us, 'I've got a lot of tricks that you guys could learn, and I really want to learn stuff from you guys.' It was sort of an unexpected but great thing to hear – that level of mutual respect. And I definitely learned a bunch of things from being in the studio with him."

Additionally, Auerbach revealed: "What we learned most from Danger Mouse was to follow our instincts, and not to be afraid to dip even further into the music we listen to that's outside the norm."

The Black Keys initially planned to record in Tennessee but decided to stay close to home. The sessions took place at Suma Studios, a two-hour drive from Akron, just outside the small city of Painesville. The facility was built inside the 80-year-old former summer home of the inventor of baby formula, William O. Frohring. The weathered studio had previously been used by Grand Funk Railroad as well as a number of Ohio acts such as Wild Cherry, Pere Ubu and Joe Walsh.

Carney recalled his state of mind before the sessions: "I was really excited. I've had this fantasy since I was 13 of going to a recording studio. I remember looking in the inside [album jackets] of the Velvet Underground's *Loaded*, or Weezer records, and seeing pictures of bands in studios, which we had never had the luxury of doing. It wasn't until our fifth record that we had that."

Meanwhile, Auerbach was forced to adjust to a dramatically different method of making music: "Brian [Burton] was very much about using ProTools as a writing tool, moving sections around on a screen. At first it was a little startling, but it was a nice change of pace, because we'd made three or four records on our own, and there's only so much you can do, recording yourself in a basement. But again, Brian's not a traditional songwriter, so it was still all about the groove."

Issued in 2008, *Attack & Release* reached the top-20. It was the first Black Keys album to be certified Gold for sales of 500,000 copies. Carney stated at the time: "We were in the middle of nowhere in Oregon, driving from Vancouver to Denver for a show. I got woken up at like 10AM by our sound engineer, who was like, 'Talk to your manager.' He got on the phone with me and was like, 'Your record went to No. 14.' To me, that was insane. It blew my mind. It was never even something that we considered happening."

One critic described the project as "spooky, sedate and moody." The album was highlighted by the track, "I Got Mine," which was a hit on mainstream and alternative rock radio and became Carney's favorite song to play in concert.

*   *   *   *   *   *

In March 2008, when the Black Keys returned to the South by Southwest music festival in Austin, Texas, there was a great deal of fan and media interest in the duo. That year, the surging duo was finally able to leave its minivan behind. Pat Carney stated at the time: "It's our first tour on a bus. It's total luxury. Having a bus makes things so less stressful. It doesn't feel like a tour. I feel like it's a vacation. If Slipknot can have a bus, why can't we?"

Graduating to mid-size concert halls, the Black Keys went on the road in May for nearly 100 shows that year. Opening some of the dates was Auerbach's protegee, singer-songwriter Jessica Lea Mayfield. Born into a musical family in Kent, Ohio, Mayfield had spent her childhood performing in her family's bluegrass band, One Way Rider, which was based in Tennessee. Auerbach later produced and played multiple instruments on Mayfield's debut album, *With Blasphemy So Heartfelt.*

Devo at the Akron Civic Theater in 2008.

On May 7, the Black Keys played a free, unadvertised "secret show" for just 150 fans at the Beachland Ballroom in Cleveland. Later, at a show in Boston, a critic wrote: "What remains remarkable... is how two skinny 20-something white guys from Akron, Ohio... can mine such deep roots and summon such soulful fire." The tour continued in Europe, Australia and New Zealand.

In the fall of 2008, the duo returned to Akron for a political fundraising concert that was staged at the city's architectural jewel – the 3,000 seat Akron Civic Theater, which had opened in 1929 as a Loew's theater. Also performing that night were

Chrissie Hynde's restaurant in Akron, the VegiTerranean.

Devo and Chrissie Hynde. This would mark the only time Akron's three most famous rock acts would appear on the same bill. Despite an energized hometown crowd, the Black Keys played a subdued set. Also that year, Auerbach would marry Stephanie Gonis. They would have one daughter.

*　　　*　　　*　　　*　　　*　　　*

After Chrissie Hynde launched an upscale vegetarian restaurant in downtown Akron, called the VegiTerranean, Dan Auerbach was asked by a reporter from *The Cleveland Plain Dealer* whether the Black Keys were also planning to open a hometown dining establishment. Auerbach joked that he was considering something in the Highland Square neighborhood: "We've been on eBay, looking at hot-dog carts. It's a dream of ours."

▶ CHAPTER 15
DAN GOES SOLO

In February 2009, the Black Keys nearly disbanded after Dan Auerbach released a solo album – purportedly without telling his musical partner, Pat Carney. Auerbach later insisted that he did inform Carney, who chose not to listen to the news.

The initial sessions for Auerbach's solo album, *Keep It Hid*, took place in late-2007 at Mark Neill's home studio in La Mesa, California. Neill was both the engineer and mixer for the project. The album was a huge departure from Auerbach's blues-inflected work in the Black Keys and was heavily influenced by his exposure to bluegrass music during his youth. David Bither, the senior vice president of Nonesuch Records, said that the album "shares DNA with the Keys even as it ventures into territory that the band would not visit."

Auerbach stated at the time: "I had a bunch of songs and just recorded them. That was pretty much it. I didn't have a plan, but I thought, I've got eight songs recorded and they sound really good, so I'll record a couple more and put out a record.

The group Drummer performing at Musica in Akron.

I definitely didn't make it for anybody but myself. I just wanted to make a record." In place of Carney, the album featured Bob Cesare on drums. Dan's father, Charles Auerbach, wrote the lyrics of the track, "Whispered Words."

Carney pursued his own side project as a member of the group, Drummer. The outfit consisted of five Ohio drummers, including Carney's longtime friend, Jamie Stillman. Although Stillman was better known as a talented guitarist, he started out as a drummer. Carney, who played bass in the group, recalled: "I figured my time would be better spent making music and doing something [more] productive than drinking Mai-Tais all winter while Dan was on tour. I called up my friend Steve [Clements] and we decided to start a band. This was in January. By June, we had the record done and a tour booked." The group's only album, *Feel Good Together*, was recorded at Tangerine Studio in Akron. The disc earned three stars in *Rolling Stone*. The reviewer called the project a '90s throwback with "wiry, hyper guitars and weird, snarly keyboards."

Auerbach and Carney both toured that year with their respective bands. Auerbach's backing group, the Fast Five, included members of the Austin-based group, Hacienda. Meanwhile, Drummer played a sold-out show at the Musica, a popular venue in downtown Akron. The five-man band was well received by the local crowd.

With the Black Keys reuniting at the end of the year, Carney had to sideline his group. He later explained: "I probably should have been more cautious with my friends [in Drummer]. We were supposed to do a West Coast tour and I had to put that on hold because the *BlakRoc* record happened. I had a kind of falling out with the lead singer and the band basically broke up. We're all on pretty good terms now, though."

*　　　*　　　*　　　*　　　*　　　*

Later in 2009, the Black Keys took a major stylistic detour with the collaborative album, *BlakRoc*. Damon Dash, a fan of the Black Keys, reached out to the duo and suggested they work together. Dash – the co-founder of the hit rap label, Roc-A-Fella Records – explained his motivation for working with the Black Keys: "It was never about, 'Let's make a rap-rock album.' It was like art – let's put this paint next to that paint and see what it looks like." Auerbach explained at the time: "All the blues music I liked was super simple and stripped down. All the hip-hop I liked was super simple and stripped down. We always heard that connection."

A number of leading rap and R&B artists appeared on the album, including Jim Jones, Raekwon, RZA, Mos Def, Ludacris, Nicole Ray and Q-Tip. Also contributing to the project was singer-songwriter, Jessica Lea Mayfield. Surprisingly, Auerbach provided few vocals: "We weren't trying to make a rap-rock record. We were trying to make a good record. When my voice was appropriate we'd give it a shot, but we were totally comfortable playing the backing band."

A *Relix* magazine writer observed some of the sessions: "Auerbach – the more verbose, often bearded, guitar-shredding Key – comes directly into the control room, straps on his bass and starts picking out a rolling, descending pattern so quickly that he's still wearing his jacket, sunglasses hung on his shirt collar. In the spare, uncluttered main studio, Carney – taller, bespectacled, quieter but more opinionated than his colleague – barely makes it onto his drum stool before beginning to thwack out a rhythm. And in a matter of moments, another example of the Black Keys credo manifests itself: Record first and ask questions later."

Auerbach described the quick pace of the sessions: "We started writing the songs in the morning, finished them in the afternoon, and the rappers came in at night. They'd spend a couple of hours working on lyrics, cut the lyrics, and that was it. Song done. Hip-hop is so alive – and it comes alive even more in that kind of environment." Amazingly, the album was completed in just eleven-days.

The project would strongly influence how the Black Keys would make their following album. Auerbach explained: "For the first time, we started all the tracks with bass and drums, and we went right from making *BlakRoc* to making *Brothers*, using the same method."

Released at the end of 2009, *BlakRoc* reached #7 on *Billboard's* Top Rap Albums chart. (A planned followup album, *BlakRoc 2*, never came to fruition even though eight-tracks had already been completed.)

During this period, Auerbach was also exposed to a great deal of '60s Southern-style soul music: "I was listening to a lot of this band called Invincibles – they're kind of like the Impressions mixed with Stax, but less Chicago and more Memphis. I got really into finding obscure soul and stuff. My soul collection must have quadrupled over the last year. I also got way into Electric Mud and the electric Howlin' Wolf stuff.... That's how I am, though. I do a lot of research and get way into things and players, and I dig – and then dig deeper. So yeah, I was listening to a lot of soul. I did the same thing when I first got into the blues.... There's still so much out there that hasn't been played, and it's so exciting to keep digging and finding inspiration."

▶ CHAPTER 16
MUSCLE SHOALS SOUND

With both Dan Auerbach and Pat Carney dealing with personal issues, they decided to record the next Black Keys album somewhere far from Akron and the Buckeye State. Around this time, Carney had ended his two-year marriage to Denise Grollmus. Auerbach recalled: "Pat had gotten divorced, he wasn't in a good place. So this record was probably more uplifting for him. [During the sessions] he could breathe a sigh of relief. He was completely separated, out of the state and able to relax a little."

Rolling Stone reported at the time: "[Carney] and his wife were married two years but together for nine, and according to pretty much everyone involved, that was about eight and a half too many.... By the end, Carney was depressed, drinking a lot, and had gained 25 pounds.... Carney finally broke it off last July, with a phone call while his wife was in Europe. He says it cost him a quarter of a million dollars, plus health insurance and a monthly alimony check: 'Totally worth it.'" In response to the *Rolling Stone* piece, Carney's ex-wife penned an article in *Salon* about their failed relationship.

The initial session for the album took place at Mark Neill's home studio in La Mesa, California – in September 2008 – during a short break in a West Coast tour. Later, the Black Keys recorded five tracks at Auerbach's studio in Akron. As both the recording engineer and co-producer, Neill suggested finishing the project at one of several studios in the South. However, *Sound On Sound* magazine reported: "[Neill recalled] 'We talked about going to Sun Studio or Sam Phillips Recording Service in Memphis, as well as Robin Hood Studios in Tyler, Texas.... Logistical problems immediately surfaced. 'Phillips was fully booked,' says Neill, 'and Sun only allowed night-time sessions because they conduct tours during the day, and I knew Dan and Pat wouldn't have any patience for that. Eventually Dan said, 'What about Muscle Shoals Sound in Alabama?' We both knew that it had been turned into a museum and hadn't been a fully functioning studio for over 30 years – it was basically a place to walk through and say, 'Wow, this is where it all happened.' That didn't deter Auerbach, who suggested that they simply bring in their own gear and use the room as-is. 'I mean, I love the sound of those old Muscle Shoals records,' says Neill, 'but I can't say that it was actually my idea to go there.'" In its heyday, the studio hosted top acts such as Duane Allman, Bob Seger, Elton John, Bob Dylan and Glenn Frey. At the facility, the Rolling Stones would record their 1971 seminal album, *Sticky Fingers*, featuring the swampy hits, "Brown Sugar" and "Wild Horses."

The Black Keys arrived at Muscle Shoals in August 2009. Carney had driven down from Akron in a rented van packed

Muscle Shoals Sound Studio in northern Alabama.

with the duo's equipment. Neill, who traveled from California, also brought some gear, including a portable mixing board. However, the once-celebrated recording studio was a relic of the past. No sessions had been staged there for thirty-years, and Neill had the arduous task of setting up a working studio.

Noel Webster, the building's owner, recalled that Auerbach had an unusual demand: "He made us take some pictures down [from the walls]. He didn't want Rod Stewart looking at him while he was recording, so that's the first thing we did was take the pictures out."

The sessions took place during the middle of a blistering hot summer inside the nearly empty, windowless, cinder-block building. Auerbach later complained that working at Muscle Shoals "was basically like returning to our basement. The shitty floors weren't supported properly, so the bass response was terrible.... But we just let the music flow. We realized that the magic is Pat and me and that can happen anywhere."

Auerbach explained how he and Carney prepared for the sessions: "We didn't talk about the album before we went into the studio. We just all showed up here on the first day, started listening to records and getting inspired by stuff – rockabilly stuff, the Cramps, the Johnny Burnette Trio and bands like Sweet, the Clash, Jonathan Richman And The Modern Lovers – all kinds of music, from all decades, but all stemming from simple, no-frills rock 'n' roll. Then we'd start jamming, something would catch our ear, and we'd build on it, consciously aiming for the simplicity of the records we were listening to."

Neill recalled how the duo quickly hit their stride: "Things were happening that were very, very transcendent, as soon as they began playing. First few takes, we literally couldn't believe what we were hearing. Dan and Pat were kind of looking at each other saying, 'That doesn't even sound like us.'" One of the tracks, "Never Give You Up," was a remake of a 1968 hit by soul singer Jerry Butler. The duo started recording a second cover song, "I'm Your Puppet," which they decided not to finish. Carney recalled: "We were halfway into it and realized, 'We can't keep doing covers. Let's go home.'"

The sessions at Muscle Shoals took just ten-days, not the full two-weeks that were scheduled. Later, Carney complained about the isolation of Muscle Shoals: "By the end, I was really starting to lose it. There isn't even really anywhere to hang out. The entire time I was there I ate at one restaurant, some barbecue place." Meanwhile, during his free time, Carney looked at online ads for apartments in New York City.

Afterward, Carney wasn't satisfied with the completed album and considered adding one additional track. Consequently, the Black Keys decided to work with producer Brian "Danger Mouse" Burton at a Brooklyn studio, the Bunker. The duo was in New York City at the time to promote the *BlakRoc* album. With a great deal of input from Burton, the Black Keys came up with the track, "Tighten Up." It was the duo's first conscious effort at recording a commercially oriented song. Auerbach later revealed: "We'd never written a hit at that point and we don't listen to the radio, so I don't even know if we were qualified to know what a hit is, frankly, at that time. Six albums in and we'd never once, ever, tried to write anything catchy. We'd always just written for fun. So that was our first attempt at writing that way."

Even after the track was completed, both Auerbach and Carney were still unsure about adding it to the album. Auerbach stated: "It was so poppy. We weren't guys who grew up listening to ABBA!" In the end, "Tighten Up" did appear on the album. Lastly, the Black Keys decided to hire Grammy winner Tchad Blake to remix the album's tracks.

▶ CHAPTER 17
NASHVILLE, TENNESSEE

Although both members of the Black Keys had publicly stated they were deeply disappointed by Devo's decision in the late-1970s to leave Akron for Los Angeles, Dan Auerbach and Pat Carney realized that living in the Rubber City wasn't particularly conducive to working in the music industry.

Auerbach insisted that he had remained in Akron for as long as he possibly could: "Every single friend that went to Firestone High School went out of town. They're gone – San Francisco, New York City. Pat and I never lived anywhere else." Likewise, Carney stated: "[Akron] was just shrinking, shrinking, shrinking, still shrinking. Living in a town [that was] going through really hard times attracting businesses to come or keeping young people around. I just remember through my 20s being adamant about never leaving Akron, because all of my friends were leaving, and then it just hit me when I was 29, I was like, 'I've gotta get... out too.'"

Carney was also motivated to leave Akron following the

The downtown skyline of Akron, Ohio.

end of his marriage. He revealed: "I felt like a hypocrite. Akron's a great town with amazing people. I'd been there for 30 years. But I was going through a divorce. I just had to move on." Carney would also cite his dislike of cold and snowy winters as another reason for leaving.

At the end of 2009, Carney moved to the Lower East Side of New York City. He said at the time, "I'm much happier here, for the most part." However, after living in a $5,000-per-month apartment in the Big Apple – one floor below actor Ryan Gosling – Carney eventually realized he had picked the wrong destination. While Akron was too cold, New York was too costly and ripe with temptation. During this period, Carney would meet a new girlfriend, Emily Ward.

Meanwhile, Auerbach wanted to move to a city with a large, established music scene. He gave serious consideration to two destinations – Nashville and New Orleans. He recalled: "Pat

The downtown skyline of Nashville at dusk.

had already left Akron. I felt I wanted a change, somewhere the winters weren't so harsh. I've been coming to Nashville since I was a kid. My dad did antique shows here a couple times a year. I would come with him. There's a rich musical tradition here, musicians who'll play music their entire lives whether they're making a living or not."

Making a visit to Nashville, Auerbach recalled: "Right after the flood [in May 2010], I went there and hung out with my buddy Patrick Keeler of the Greenhornes and Raconteurs. He showed me around." While exploring the city, Auerbach met with David Ferguson, who was best known as the recording engineer of Johnny Cash's final four albums. Auerbach recalled: "[Ferguson] was one of the first people I ever met in Nashville. He introduced me to everybody – Merle Haggard,

Del McCoury, John Prine, Cowboy Jack. He opened this world up to me, and I'll be forever thankful to him for that. But it's the reason why I came to Nashville. It was like my *Field Of Dreams*, really. And [Ferguson has] been that person to kind of open the door for me."

In August, Auerbach left Ohio for Tennessee. He explained at the time: "I didn't want to go to New York and I didn't want to go to Los Angeles. I didn't want to go anywhere so soft you didn't have seasons, because I like seasons. So, Nashville it was. It has a slight chill in the winter, even some snow sometimes. And it still felt like Akron because I live in a neighborhood where there's sidewalks and kids playing." More importantly, he insisted: "I moved to Nashville... because it was Music City. I built my studio right down the street from the Station Inn, the world-famous bluegrass spot. You know, it's always been about music. It's always been about being in a room and the interaction between the musicians."

Just two-months later, in October, Auerbach received a surprise announcement: "Pat was living in New York City and then one day, out of the blue, he was like, 'I'm moving to Nashville!' He literally moved right down the street from me."

Carney explained: "I'm the kind of person who, if I'm at a restaurant, I'll just say, 'I'll have what he's ordering.' That's pretty much how I got to Nashville. The same thing happened when I moved to New York from Akron. I was going through a divorce and I wanted to spread my wings a little bit. I never thought I'd live in New York but my brother Mike was moving there, so I basically tagged along. Then after about a year, Dan decided to leave Akron and move to Nashville. I was having a little too much fun in New York. So I just tagged along. Pretty much ordered what he ordered."

While Auerbach settled into a modest home, Carney eventually purchased what a journalist described as "a sprawling, almost castlelike stucco structure modeled after a French farmhouse."

Michael Carney, Patrick's brother, observed: "It's kind of interesting that [their move to Nashville] happened to coincide with their first record to kind of get huge. I look at it as kind of a new chapter in the story of the Black Keys. You get to a point where you realize what you're inputting into your brain or your eyes or your ears is influencing what you're outputting. Your environment influences what you do. A lot. I think Dan and Pat know that." (Chuck and Mary Auerbach later moved to Nashville to be closer to their son. But after a five-year stay, they decided to return to Akron.)

Nashville is best known as the capital of country music and the home of the Grand Ole Opry. In the two decades after World War II, the sleepy city emerged as a music industry powerhouse. In the 1970 book, *The Nashville Sound,* author Paul Hemphill wrote: "Suddenly, old Nashville, has become the second-largest recording center in the world, only a step behind New York. Scheduling their first recording session at 10AM and finishing their last one of the day at one o'clock the next morning, the city's 40 recording studios (five-years ago there were only ten) produce more 45rpm 'single' records than any city in the world. In Nashville there are more than 1,500 union musicians and an equal number of songwriters, served by 29 talent agencies, seven record plants, 400 music-publishing houses, 53 record companies, offices for three performance rights organizations, and seven trade papers."

During the 1950s and '60s, a number of rock and roll acts began recording in Nashville. At RCA's Studio B, the Everly Brothers recorded a string of radio hits and Elvis Presley recorded "Heartbreak Hotel" and 200 other songs. Owen Bradley's Quonset Hut was the site of notable recording sessions by Johnny Cash and Patsy Cline as well as the early rock standard, "Be-Bop-A-Lulu" by Gene Vincent. And in 1969, Bob Dylan recorded his seminal album, *Nashville Skyline*, at Columbia Studios.

In 1974, Paul McCartney spent a few months in the city, writing songs and rehearsing with Wings for an upcoming tour. He said at the time: "It's one of the most musical cities in the world, and the only one with the quality to be the music capital. Tennesseans are real downhome folks, down to earth, and the musicians are fantastic." By the turn of the century, Nashville emerged as a booming metropolis and tourist destination that attracted six-million visitors a year.

▶ CHAPTER 18

THE BLUES BROTHERS

At the start of 2010, Pat Carney stated: "I imagine Dan and I will never have that problem of having to deal with extreme success. We've had a gradual upwards – I guess – trajectory. I think we're both smart enough to know that it won't last forever." However, in a matter of months, the duo's fortunes would reach heights that neither member could have imagined.

In May, the Black Keys released their sixth album, *Brothers*. To the duo's chagrin, the album had already been leaked online. As for the album's title, Dan Auerbach revealed: "Pat and I have spent more time together than with anybody in our families. We understand each other better than anybody on Earth. We love each other, we get on each other's nerves, we piss each other off. But like brothers, we know it's all OK."

Rolling Stone magazine writer David Fricke said of the album: "*Brothers* was classic Muscle Shoals – taut, rough blues and churning funk wrapped in reverb shadows and lyric turbulence – jolted forward by the Black Keys' airtight garage-band modernism."

The album's lead-off single, "Tighten Up," was a surprise breakthrough hit. After returning to the U.S. after a brief European tour, Carney stated: "Our manager told us that 'Tighten Up' was getting played a lot in America. It was in the Top-20 on the Alternative Songs charts, which had never happened to us. Then by October, it was No. 1 [for 10 weeks].... That song completely changed our lives. We... almost didn't put it on the record and spent the whole time we were doing it drinking beer and eating chicken wings." The track was also the duo's first chart entry on *Billboard's* Hot 100.

The song's oddball music video also attracted attention. Auerbach recalled: "It's like a Laurel and Hardy skit, basically. Both of us are at the park with our kids. They start trying to show off for some girls and start fighting, and we have to break it up. But then one of the kids' hot moms comes over, and we start competing over her. It ends with us fighting in the sandbox and the kids standing over us, shaking their heads." The clip later won an MTV Video Music Award in the Breakthrough Video category. However, when Auerbach and Carney received their MTV Moon Man statuettes, the metal plaques on the awards read "Black Eyed Peas" – not the Black Keys.

Brothers spawned a second significant radio hit, "Howlin' For You." An upbeat, bluesy, guitar-driven love song, it later appeared in numerous television shows, feature films and commercials. The song's unusual music video was a parody of a film trailer and featured Tricia Helfer (from *Battlestar Galactica*), Todd Bridges (from *Diff'rent Strokes*), championship snowboarder Shaun White and fashion model Diora Baird. Meanwhile, Auerbach and Carney were billed as

"Las Teclas de Negro" – which was Spanish for "The Keys of Black." The clip was nominated in the category of Best Rock Video in the 2011 MTV Video Music Awards. The album's other notable tracks included "Next Girl," "Ten Cent Pistol" and "Everlasting Light."

Brothers debuted at #3 on the *Billboard* sales chart. Later certified Platinum, it was the best-selling alternative-rock album of the year. Additionally, the Black Keys were named Artist of the Year by *Spin* magazine, and an *Esquire* magazine headline read: "Are the Black Keys the Best Rock Band in America?" And a music critic for *The Tampa Bay Times* observed: "No longer are the Black Keys just a scruffy singer and gangly drummer screaming and walloping like two teenagers in the basement. They're two of America's biggest rock stars, and with every album, they're acting more and more like it.... Strangely, nothing about the Black Keys' first 10 years indicated they were on their way to this kind of superstardom. Critics and bloggers swooned for their distorted, punkish blues; tunes like 'Your Touch' and 'I Got Mine' popped up in films, commercials and TV shows. But as much as their music grabbed you and shook you, it never felt remotely like stadium rock. *Brothers* changed all that."

Just as quickly, the Black Keys graduated to larger venues to meet ticket demand. Nicole Atkins, the opening act on their 2010 tour, recalled: "When things started happening with that album, they happened fast. We went out with them when *Brothers* first came out, and we were playing big shows to about 2,500 people. Within a matter of months, we're suddenly playing to crowds between 8,000 and 10,000. It was crazy to see that happen." Auerbach stated at the time: "We used to tour without any lights or any of that crap, but now we have to do it. But we're putting on the same exact show we would in front of 100 people." The band's lighting system was supervised by the duo's oldest employee, Mike Grant, who had first joined the Black Keys when they were still touring the country in a crowded minivan.

In 2010, the red-hot duo played nearly 110 shows. Wanting to recreate the studio arrangements of their songs from *Brothers*, the two members of the Black Keys were augmented onstage by a pair of backing musicians, bassist Nick Movshon and keyboardist Leon Michels. On July 27, the Black Keys performed for a large audience at New York's Central Park. A *New York Times* music critic observed: "Mr. Michels and Mr. Movshon brought a distressed midrange and a murky bottom end to the group's sound, and for the purposes of these songs, it worked. But they were appendages rather than part of the band's core, and it's unclear how long such an arrangement can last."

A serious problem arose during the tour. Carney experienced a massive panic attack while performing at the Lollapalooza festival in Chicago. (Also on the bill at the three-day event were Devo and Chrissie Hynde.) Carney recalled: "It was perfect conditions for a panic attack, which I've never had before. I was tired, I hadn't really eaten that day, I'd had a lot of coffee, the sun was setting right in my face, tons of people, and a record that was... really resonating. I thought I was going to pass out, right during the first song. And it didn't go away, the whole set. And it didn't go away for months afterwards. I had to go to this hypnotist, and he fixed it."

Although the hypnosis alleviated his stage fright, Carney

was left with a new problem that he blamed on the treatments – sleepwalking. Subsequently, Carney received some helpful advice from his father: "If you're stressed all the time, what a waste."

*　　　*　　　*　　　*　　　*　　　*

The Black Keys had a long history of licensing their music, beginning with "Set You Free" from 2003's *Thickfreakness*. The duo enjoyed a great deal of publicity when the track was featured in a commercial for Nissan. Dan Auerbach insisted at the time: "We're not going to let just anybody use our music. We've turned a bunch of people down and will continue to do so. But it's good exposure for us. I mean, nobody plays us on the radio, and there's no such thing as MTV anymore."

Similarly, Patrick Carney explained: "When no one's buying your records, it's easy to justify selling a song. But once you start selling records, you can't really justify having two songs in Cadillac commercials. It looks greedy. And it is greedy. This whole music thing should be about music."

The Black Keys' songs have appeared in spots for American Express, Victoria's Secret, Cadillac, Subaru and BMW. However, they turned down a number of offers, including £200,000 ($320,000) for the use of a song in a British commercial for Hellmann's mayonnaise. They later regretted their decision. The duo's songs also began appearing in films. Auerbach remarked: "I really always get a kick out of going to movies and hearing one of our songs in this big... multimillion dollar movie, knowing that we recorded the song in our basement for, like, 20 dollars."

In 2012, *Billboard* magazine reported: "The group gets about one... offer each day, both for new music and older material. Black Keys manager John Peets of Q Prime Nashville, who handles the requests in-office, describes the volume of licensing inquiries as 'shocking.' 'They write such strong hooks – that's why they've been successful with licensing,' Peets says. 'Most people think about synchs in terms of complete songs, but really, it's more about which 30-second snippets will work.'"

However, when the Black Keys became more selective about licensing their songs in commercials, a number of advertisers began using sound-alike tracks, which resulted in the duo launching legal actions against Home Depot and Pizza Hut. Both lawsuits were settled out of court.

▶ CHAPTER 19
ON TOP OF THE WORLD

The Black Keys opened 2011 by taking full control of their career path. Pat Carney recalled: "We were supposed to go to Australia for a month and then Europe for two months, but we canned the whole... tour. We paid $200,000 to promoters to *not* go on tour. That was most of the money that we'd made the previous year. But we just thought, 'We're going to go home, and we're going to go make a record. That's what we like to do. We don't want to do this shit.' And we went and made *El Camino*. Everyone was like... 'You could have toured that record [*Brothers*] for another two years if you wanted.' I've never looked at it like that."

In January, the Black Keys made their first appearance on *Saturday Night Live*, on an episode hosted by comedian Jim Carrey. It was Mark Mothersbaugh's former girlfriend Laraine Newman who encouraged *SNL* producer Lorne Michaels to book the duo. On the program, the Black Keys performed

"Howlin' For You" and "Tighten Up." Carney recalled the stress of performing on *SNL*: "It's like the biggest American TV kind of thing for a rock band... And yeah, it was terrifying, to be honest. Because all my friends and family were watching it, and it was live, so you could really screw it up and everyone would know. But when we finished the second song, I've never felt that accomplished before." The Black Keys were the first Northeastern Ohio act to perform on the program since Canton native Macy Gray in 2001.

The following month, the Black Keys made another television appearance after they were nominated for a pair of Grammys. At the time, Carney recalled a conversation he had while traveling on the Ohio Turnpike: "I remember driving back from a gig in Toledo in 2002, and Dan's dad asked us if we ever thought we'd be nominated for a Grammy. I laughed at him for an hour and a half." Carney wasn't laughing when he attended the 53rd annual Grammy Awards ceremony at the Staples Center in Los Angeles.

Before the ceremony, Carney stated: "I think it's kind of weird. I never thought we would get nominated for a Grammy. I have been having kind of anxiety dreams about it. I keep having dreams that we lose all the Grammys.... We'll see what happens. I think maybe the only way we will win something is if we, like, witness the head of the Grammys murder somebody. He'd owe us."

At the ceremony, both members of the Black Keys were treated as outsiders and received little media attention. Carney recalled: "When we walked the red carpet, everyone pushed us out of the way so that Kim Kardashian and Snooki could get through."

In a radical departure from how they usually dressed, both members of the Black Keys were smartly attired in black tuxes. They won their first Grammy of the night in the category of Best Alternative Rock Album for *Brothers*. Taking the podium, the duo acknowledged Akron and thanked their family, friends and record company in a very brief speech.

Later in the evening, when they won a second Grammy for their hit single, "Tighten Up" – in the Best Rock Performance category – the duo took their time walking to the podium. Taking the microphone, Auerbach said: "Sorry about that. We were in the back of the class. We'd like to thank, um, the same people we thanked last time." Additionally, Michael Carney – Pat's brother, who designed the cover of *Brothers* – won the prize for Best Recording Package. The CD was manufactured with heat-sensitive ink that changed color when heated. Later, Auerbach and Carney both looked overwhelmed as they held up their Grammys for the press.

Over the next year, the Black Keys continued to receive accolades. In addition to their Grammy wins, *Rolling Stone* magazine named *Brothers* the number-two album of the year! Also, a critic at *The Word* proclaimed that "The Black Keys are so hot it hurts, with everyone from Thom Yorke to Raekwon singing their praises." Robert Plant also emerged as an outspoken fan of the group. The former Led Zeppelin frontman stated the Black Keys were "a beacon for hard-hitting music – which is just blues and attitude. When you go from one section of a song into the next, there's only the drums to steer you, and Patrick does a great job creating those hypnotic moments. They lean toward Charley Patton one minute, then they're off in another direction." Auerbach later commented: "I think Robert

Plant and I probably listened to the same music growing up – blues music and American roots music. When we get together, we talk about that stuff."

Years later, Auerbach would observe: "I still think *Brothers* is the best-sounding record we've ever done. We didn't see any of the huge sales and Grammys coming, but it was the first time that the sound we heard in our heads was finally there. Finally we got the lo-fi, distorted... sound that we loved so much, but hi-fi at the same time. I love the simplicity of it. I think the enthusiasm shows on every level of *Brothers*."

In November, the Black Keys were the musical guests on *Saturday Night Live* for a second time in one year – a very rare occurrence. On the program, they unleashed confident performances of "Gold On The Ceiling" and "Lonely Boy."

*   *   *   *   *   *

Dan Auerbach's primary motivation for settling in Nashville was his desire to work with the city's many legendary musicians. In September 2010, he paid $280,000 for a building that had previously housed a call center. Inside the unassuming structure, Auerbach constructed a recording studio, which he named Easy Eye Sound. Feeling somewhat guilty about his enormous success, he sold his classic convertible after opening the studio.

In the studio's main room, Auerbach stored his impressive collection of vinyl LPs, which were neatly organized on several shelves. He adorned the walls with framed photographs of musical legends – country music pioneer Bill Monroe, blues legend Muddy Waters and Akron's own Devo. The wall of a comfortable lounge area was accentuated by a psychedelic-styled poster of the 1967 biker film, *The Wild Rebels*. A *Rolling Stone* reporter wrote: "The lounge also features two vintage motorcycles next to a wall of biker-gang jackets, a wraparound couch, stuffed animals, shelves of rock and roll books and several Grammys." And on the wall of the control room, Auerbach placed a flag from the Isle of Man in order to celebrate his mother's British ancestry. The facility also included a well-stocked bar.

Additionally, Auerbach had amassed a few dozen guitars. He admitted: "I'm not too picky about guitars. I love to collect them, mostly oddballs, but I'm not married to any brand or model. Whatever guitar has the best character for the song is the one I want to use, because if you've got a style you're going to sound like yourself no matter what guitar you play." Although the studio also featured various pianos and keyboards, Auerbach had one favorite: "I've got an old piano that I pulled out of a basement in Ohio that I've had for a decade and I love it. It's sort of become the signature piano sound in the studio. It's got a real, special, weird thing going on."

The centerpiece of the facility was a vintage API 1604 mixing board that Auerbach had purchased from Evergreen State College in Olympia, Washington. He stated at the time: "Having a place that's tailor made for you is a real luxury. Everything here works... All you need to do is pull up a fader on the console to start recording. You see a lot of studio web sites and think they've got cool shit. Then when you show up half of it's not working. If it doesn't work in my studio it doesn't stay on the floor."

Eventually, Auerbach used the studio to record a growing

list of artists such as Jessica Lea Mayfield, Robert Finley, Hacienda, the Growlers and Nikki Lane. Auerbach would also launch his own record label – also called Easy Eye Sound.

▶ CHAPTER 20
EL CAMINO BLUES

While recording the followup to *Brothers*, Dan Auerbach and Pat Carney wondered if they could repeat their success. Auerbach recalled: "I'm sure we felt a little bit of pressure, but we didn't let it direct us. We just kind of went in the studio and did our thing. We just tried to have fun and enjoy ourselves, really. That was the only goal. And to try and make a good record, to write catchy songs." While making the album, the duo drew inspiration by listening to albums by the Clash, the Akron-based band, the Cramps, and a number of 1950s rockabilly guitarists.

During the sessions, Auerbach and Carney received a great deal of assistance from Brian "Danger Mouse" Burton. Carney recalled: "He basically asked if he could be co-writer on the album, and there was pretty much no discussion whatsoever. 'If you want to do it, of course.' He's probably the only person at this point that we trust 100 percent in the studio." Auerbach agreed: "I mean, it's weird. I've never written lyrics with anyone before, so sometimes it was infuriating, sometimes it was really awesome and really easy. But it was definitely different." In addition to co-writing the songs, Burton also played keyboards and co-produced the album.

The project was recorded over a two-month period at Easy Eye Studio. Auerbach explained: "We wanted *El Camino* to be very simple, no real album effects, just drums, bass, guitar, organ; that's it. No studio trickery. It's certainly a studio album, but we didn't want... anything that isn't just a band playing live."

However, the sessions were more challenging than expected. Auerbach revealed: "It was difficult at times. Some days it worked great. Some days it was just infuriating. You gotta lose any kind of insecurity. It was a totally different way of thinking for me." The Black Keys spent a great deal of time working on the structure of the songs – something they had never done in the past. Auerbach explained: "We were getting into the nuances of each song by asking ourselves, 'How long should this intro be? How long should the pre-chorus be? Should there even be a pre-chorus?' We were playing with tempos and BPMs, seeing how a vocal hook does or doesn't work at a faster speed. And usually, we went with the faster option."

Auerbach also revealed: "This record was way more about melody and less about lyrical content. The lyrics had to fit into the little square we created for the melody. We didn't want to take a year making it, so I was coming up with lyrics that fit into the melody and doing it fast." However, even after the project was completed, Burton kept trying to convince Auerbach to change the lyrics on some of the songs. Auerbach said at the time: "We're all perfectionists, but Brian is still trying to get me to change those words. I'm like, '*Dude*, come on! I'm over it. Let's just go make another record or something.'" In the end, Auerbach proclaimed: "This is our first pure rock 'n' roll album. We kept it very simple and ripped through it in just 40 days."

On the eve of the release of *El Camino* in December 2011, Carney was anxious about how the album would be received: "We've had people say: 'You're going to be the biggest band in America in six months.' I guess that's possible. But we could also be made fun of everywhere. 'Cos everything's fickle. I don't pay attention to it. I think Danger Mouse would tell us that we have a fear of success. That's probably true. I just worried so much about not being good enough. Maybe that's an Akron thing. I wasn't raised super-poor, but my parents got divorced, and my mother didn't have much money. Even now if I have a cake, I'll eat it slowly, and I save most of the money I have. I rent a BMW, I buy shit from the mall."

Despite the title of the album, the vehicle pictured on the front cover was not an El Camino but a 1994 Plymouth Grand Voyager. Auerbach told *Rolling Stone* magazine, "It's not the exact van, but it's similar to the one that we toured in for two years when we started the band. All the gear fit behind the rear bench, and we took the middle seats out so we could sleep on the floor." Carney's father had originally paid $4,000 for the used vehicle. It was retired after 190,000 miles and resold. Although the photo of the van confused some of the duo's fans, Carney revealed, "That's the reaction we were going for. It

A classic El Camino, manufactured by Chevrolet.

didn't work in Europe because they don't know what an El Camino is over there."

Meanwhile, the album's first single was a surprise hit. Carney recalled: "We let the label pick the single and they picked 'Lonely Boy.' Honestly, we didn't know if people were going to like it at all. We were shocked when people liked it."

Although their label had allocated $80,000 for a promotional video, the members of the Black Keys were not happy with the final result. The elaborate clip had been filmed in multiple locations and featured actor Bob Odenkirk. As *Billboard* magazine reported: "Instead of releasing the big-budget video they shot for 'Lonely Boy,' the Keys opted for footage of a security guard named Derrick Tuggle, who epitomizes the idea of dancing like no one's watching. Finding and recording Tuggle, originally hired as an extra, was essentially an accident, but the video fit in perfectly with the 'inside joke' theme of the album's viral-heavy marketing." Remarkably, the bare-bones video for "Lonely Boy" – which was filmed in a single take – became an instant sensation. Overnight, Tuggle became a media star and appeared on numerous talk shows.

Another radio hit, "Gold On The Ceiling," quickly became a fan favorite. Featuring fuzz guitar, the retro-style glam-rocker reached number-two on *Billboard's* Alternative Rock chart. The duo released two different videos for the track. The album's most difficult track to record was "Little Black Submarines." In the end, the duo simply combined two different takes. Opening as a soft ballad, the song transitions to an electric, hard-pounding rocker in a style reminiscent of Led Zeppelin. However, Auerbach insisted: "It's accidental if anything. I've never even owned a Led Zeppelin album." One critic humorously said about the song: "They don't make vintage folk-rock heavy metal like they used to – if they ever used to." Another track, "Weight Of Love," was reminiscent of classic Pink Floyd.

Although the album was initially slated for release in September, it was belatedly issued on December 6, 2011. As a gag, the Black Keys placed an advertisement for the minivan featured on the cover in their hometown paper. In part, the ad read: "1994 El Camino: 273,000 mi. 200 cubic-in.... Priced to sell – Grab the Keys and go! Contact Pat or Dan."

Over the next several weeks, the album would receive mostly glowing reviews in the rock press. One reviewer pointed out the project's rock-oriented sound: "When times are as good as they are on *El Camino,* the blues can wait for another day." Another wrote: "It's a summer record released in the winter, a dance record that just happens to be rock, a rock record that fans of LCD Soundsystem will dig. It's a party record, a driving down the highway, 'I'm in love with rock and roll, and I'll be out all night' record." And the project earned four stars in *Rolling Stone*, with a reviewer proclaiming, "The Akron, Ohio, guys brought raw, riffed-out power back to pop's lexicon.... *El Camino* is the Keys' grandest pop gesture yet, augmenting dark-hearted fuzz blasts with sleekly sexy choruses and Seventies-glam flair."

Several days after the release of the album, Auerbach and Carney were guests on an episode of the Travel Channel program, *No Reservations*, which was hosted by celebrity chef Anthony Bourdain. He opened the show by calling Akron "a known breeding ground for serial killers," which was a reference to Jeffrey Dahmer, who was raised in suburban Akron.

On the program, the duo picked up Bourdain in the same beat-up minivan featured on the cover of *El Camino*. Soon after, the two Akronites were schooled on a variety of barbecued meats from various Kansas City restaurants. While enjoying his meal, Carney admitted to Bourdain: "When we first started touring, we had $5 a day that we could spend on food."

Meanwhile, earlier that same day, the Black Keys learned that *El Camino* had sold an impressive 206,000 copies in its first week. The album would reach number-two on the charts, and blocked from the top spot by a Michael Bublé Christmas album. To celebrate their success, Auerbach and Carney bought a bottle of pricey, 20-year-old Pappy Van Winkle bourbon, which they shared with Bourdain.

El Camino became the best-selling studio album of the

Black Keys' career, with around 1.5 million copies purchased in the U.S. *El Camino* was ranked number-twelve on *Rolling Stone* magazine's list of the year's top albums.

▶ CHAPTER 21
AT THE GRAMMYS

On January 19, 2012, the Black Keys graced the cover of *Rolling Stone* for the first time. In the magazine, Pat Carney famously stated that "rock and roll is dying because people became OK with Nickelback being the biggest band in the world." During the middle of their interview, the Black Keys were informed that they had sold out Madison Square Garden in just 15-minutes.

Later, Nickelback issued a response to Carney's statement: "Thanks to the drummer in the Black Keys calling us the Biggest Band in the World in *Rolling Stone*. Hehe." However, Carney followed with another comment during an interview with MTV News: "I mean, look, I've got a lot of friends and not one of them has a Nickelback record. I'm not like a small minority.... I didn't mean to single them out, actually. It just came out. There's much worse bands than Nickelback. Maybe."

Hitting the road to promote *El Camino*, the Black Keys would play more than 100 shows in 2012, headlining arena-sized venues. One writer observed: "Arenas suit the Black Keys, another unlikely feat for this onetime niche band on a big winning streak." In order to better recreate their music on a concert stage, Auerbach and Carney were again joined by a pair of backing musicians.

Despite their breakthrough success, neither member of the Black Keys adopted a traditional rock star lifestyle. Auerbach explained: "I think the mainstream public.... they want a rock star who acts like a rock star.... And we don't act like that. And I think it kind of hurts us some ways.... A lot of writers, I think, don't take us seriously... because we're just too normal."

Meanwhile, at the 55th annual Grammy Awards in February, the Black Keys swept all three rock awards. One of the prizes was presented by Ohio native Dave Grohl. Marcus Mumford, the vocalist of the band Mumford & Sons, said at the time: "We figured we weren't going to win anything because the Black Keys have been sweeping up all day, rightfully so."

After receiving an award for the track, "Lonely Boy," Auerbach gave a short speech, thanking a number of individuals and record companies as well as "everybody in Akron, Ohio, everybody in Nashville, Tennessee." Taking the stage for a rendition of "Lonely Boy," the Black Keys were joined by Dr. John and the Preservation Hall Jazz Band. Remarkably, Auerbach won a fourth Grammy that same night – in the Producer of the Year category.

Carney, meanwhile, was unhappy about the increasingly non-rock stance of the Grammy Awards: "We're going to be playing music onstage with all this pop music and stuff that has nothing to do with what we're about. But we couldn't say no.... But we had to sit through the Grammy performances before [going onstage]. And it was atrocious. I mean, it really is like so alienating." Carney also stated that he had no desire to ever perform at the Grammys again.

After the ceremony, the Black Keys were mobbed by reporters. During the commotion, Carney inadvertently started a skirmish with teen idol Justin Bieber. When asked if Bieber had been snubbed by the Grammys, Carney replied: "He's rich, right? Grammys are for music, not for money... And he's making a lot of money. He should be happy." In response, 18-year-old Bieber tweeted: "The Black Keys drummer should be slapped around haha." Almost immediately, Carney was targeted by an online army of Bieber fans.

Carney later explained: "With regards to the Bieber thing, it was the most frightening day of our career and also one of the most exhilarating. We knew a lot of people had no idea what our music sounded like and then afterwards we celebrated for a little bit and then I have a TMZ camera asking me about Justin Bieber. The last thing I would ever expect to happen was a camera in my face, followed by a camera in my face asking me about someone who I know nothing about."

*   *   *   *   *   *

Also in 2012, Dan Auerbach worked with another of his musical idols, 71-year-old New Orleans legend, Dr. John (a.k.a. Mac Rebennack). Dr. John recalled: "I think it was very mystical how this all came together. Before I ever heard of the Black Keys, my granddaughter gave me one of their records. Then the next thing I know, Dan calls me out of the blue."

Dr. John was initially leery about working with someone

half his age. Auerbach recalled: "He wouldn't commit. I called him and told him how much of a fan I was and how I wanted to make a record, but he just blew me off. He was like, 'Call me back next Tuesday...' He would talk in this much thicker accent when he was on the phone. I later found out that [it] was his defense mechanism – when he doesn't know somebody, he... mumbles! When I flew to his house and he let me in, he started talking normally. He went into his room and got me his notebook which had all the lyrics for the record... and that was that."

Soon after, Auerbach produced Dr. John's album, *Locked Down*, at Easy Eye Sound in Nashville. Auerbach recalled: "We were listening to a lot of 45s when we were making that record." One reviewer wrote: "Black Keys fans coming to this record have a few 'a-ha' moments in store when they realize where some of Auerbach's stylings have come from. Dr. John fans, meanwhile, may find that this record... adds yet another plume to his ornate headdress." The project was ranked number-fifteen on *Rolling Stone's* list of the top albums of 2012 and earned a Grammy in the category of Best Blues Album. Dr. John and the Black Keys also performed together at the prestigious Bonnaroo Festival in Tennessee.

Meanwhile, Carney married Emily Ward in a ceremony that took place in the backyard of their home in Nashville, before 350 guests. The couple walked down the aisle to the 1968 pop chestnut, "Crimson And Clover" by Tommy James and the Shondells. Comedian and *Saturday Night Live* cast member, Will Forte, officiated the ceremony.

▶ CHAPTER 22
TURN BLUE WITH GHOULARDI

In 2012, Auerbach revealed how he composed music: "I wasn't even thinking about songwriting on the early records, just music and the groove. It was absolutely just [messing] around – taking old blues riffs, making up lyrics on the spot, and turning it into a song. Then we started sort of digging into these records that we love, and trying to figure out why it is we love them so much, besides the sonics." Later, he would write down ideas for lyrics in a notebook.

Auerbach also discussed the Black Keys' approach in the studio: "We never rehearse, we never practice. We make a record, and it'll be what it's going to be. We've always done that. We feel that it's really important to get the first or second take, and not try to perfect it, which can ruin the soul of a song or the original intent. You can beat a horse to death when you're in a studio. We try to avoid that. When you're too comfortable with a song, it's going to feel like that on the record. Like you're not taking your risks."

Meanwhile, the Black Keys started their next album in January 2013, during a break in the hectic El Camino tour. Once again, Brian "Danger Mouse" Burton was hired as the co-producer. The initial sessions took place at the Key Club in Benton Harbor, Michigan. Auerbach and Carney wanted to record at the facility in order to use Sly Stone's old mixing board – a rare custom-built Flickinger. The duo learned about the studio from the members of the band, the Kills. Auerbach and Carney spent twelve-days at the facility and slept in a room above the studio.

Auerbach recalled: "We went to Michigan to knock everything out that was on the top of our heads, just every idea that came we put it down." For the sessions, Auerbach mostly played a much-abused 1964 Fender Stratocaster that he borrowed from a member of the Mescaleros. Years earlier, the instrument had belonged to Sid Vicious of the Sex Pistols. He had received the guitar as a gift from Joe Strummer of the Clash. Unfortunately, the Key Club sessions were not especially productive. In the end, only a few of the songs would appear on the duo's album – including a portion of the track, "Fever."

Following a short tour across South America, the Black Keys went back to work in the studio. However, Auerbach was having trouble focusing on the sessions due to turmoil in his personal life. He had separated from his wife of four-years, Stephanie Gonis. After a messy breakup that was marred by various accusations, he eventually agreed to pay a $5 million divorce settlement. With details of their marital woes reported in the press, Auerbach stated at the time: "When you reach a certain level [of success], nothing is private anymore. We just have to accept that we're at that level now."

Although the Black Keys had allotted two-weeks for the sessions at Easy Eye Sound, Auerbach and Carney quit after just one day. *Rolling Stone* reported: "Burton flew home the next day. Auerbach took a rare vacation, riding a 1937 Harley Davidson to North Carolina on a camping trip with friends." (Auerbach was a collector of vintage motorcycles, many of which were later displayed at the Lane Motor Museum in Nashville.)

After returning to Nashville, Auerbach was forced to deal with the aftermath of his divorce: "I definitely did not know which way was up. It was like *Spinal Tap*, all of my emotions were at 11. At that time I was a full-time dad. [My daughter] was not in school, and I was living in a one-bedroom apartment with her, so I had way bigger shit to think about than the music."

Four months later, Auerbach spent a week in New York City, working on some solo tracks. Soon after, he regrouped with Carney and Burton, this time at Sunset Sound Recorders in Los Angeles. At the legendary facility, the duo used a vintage, top-of-the-line Neve mixing board that had once belonged to Steely Dan. However, Auerbach was not a fan of the Neve board.

In the wake of his difficult divorce, Auerbach revealed at the time: "It was the first time that I've ever used music therapeutically. I've been pretty lucky in life. But this year definitely tested me. It made me realize how lucky I am to have music in my life and to be able to go into the studio, to have all these musicians as friends who can come in and play music with me. It's awesome, you know?" Consequently, much of the album's lyrics reflected his emotional state at the time. After recording what would become the album's opening track, "Weight Of Love," Auerbach had a creative breakthrough and was able to complete the rest of the album's tracks. The duo would spend four-weeks at the studio in Los Angeles.

After some fine tuning at Auerbach's Easy Eye Sound, the album was finally completed in February 2014. Auerbach recalled: "It was such a relief to finish the record and close that chapter. I was just so happy to be done with it and have it behind me. There was both a sense of achievement and one of absolute relief." However, he didn't feel confident about the completed album: "It's not an instantly gratifying record of quick, fast pop songs like *El Camino* was. But over the course of years and decades hopefully it's going to be as pleasing as a record like this can be."

*   *   *   *   *   *

The eighth Black Keys studio album, *Turn Blue,* was named after a catchphrase that was popularized by Ghoulardi – an outrageous late-night horror-movie personality on Cleveland television in the 1960s. As the host of *Shock Theater*, Ghoulardi (real name Ernie Anderson) puffed away on a cigarette, spouted off-the-wall beatnik poetry, rode his motorcycle through the studio and blew up props – all while blasting mostly obscure rock and jazz music. A number of

Cleveland and Akron rock acts have cited the host as an influence. Auerbach stated: "I think all of our favorite bands from Ohio were heavily influenced by Ghoulardi: The Cramps, Tin Huey, Pere Ubu, Devo, Dead Boys. You read interviews with them and they're all talking about growing up watching the show when they were 13 years old. So in a weird way, I think we were influenced by something we never even saw."

Ghoulardi also played a role in shaping the creative outlook of Akron-raised film director Jim Jarmusch, who proclaimed: "Ghoulardi was a great influence, especially as I get older and look back on my youth. He had this kind of anarchism and wildness. He'd look into the camera and say, 'Camera 4 you're ugly.' He had all the spiel, the frightwig and goatee and the dark glasses with one eye punched out. The way he had all this reverb on his voice. He was such a non-conformist inspiration.... As a kid growing up in Akron I never saw anyone or anything like that. He was an anti-conformist weirdo." Jarmusch added: "So yeah, if you ask anyone who grew up in Northeastern Ohio in the '60s, we're all familiar with Ghoulardi and his influence on us. I think Chrissie Hynde still has her original Ghoulardi T-shirt." A controversial and outspoken figure, Ghoulardi was forced off the airwaves in 1966, despite his remarkably high ratings. He relocated to Los Angeles and became the on-air voice of the ABC television network.

Meanwhile, *Turn Blue* was finally released on May 13, 2014. It was the duo's first number-one album on *Billboard* magazine – and also the first-ever number-one for Nonesuch Records in its entire 50-year history. In its first week of release, the album barely outsold Michael Jackson's posthumously released project, *Xscape*, which had to settle for the number-two spot. The Black Keys performed two songs from the album on *Saturday Night Live* – "Fever" and "Bullet In The Brain."

Meanwhile, *Rolling Stone* gave the album four and a half stars, with the reviewer writing: "*Turn Blue* is a genuine turning point – into a decisively original rock, with a deeper shade of blues. You still get the minimalist vigor of the Keys' first records." Another critic observed: "*Turn Blue* is soaked in soul texture, saturated in wine-rich atmosphere. It rarely drives the speed limit. Instead, Auerbach's lyrics obsess over a broken relationship, and the music sinks into darkness. Key to the transition is producer Brian 'Danger Mouse' Burton."

The album's first single, "Fever," featured Burton on the synthesizer. In the song's music video, Dan Auerbach portrayed a televangelist pleading for donations, with Patrick Carney sitting at his side. The video was directed by Theo Wenner, the son of *Rolling Stone* magazine founder, Jann Wenner.

Additionally, the album spawned the radio hits, "Gotta Get Away," "Weight Of Love" and "Turn Blue." The project earned three Grammy nominations – *Turn Blue* for Best Rock Album and "Fever" for Best Rock Performance and Best Rock Song.

▶ CHAPTER 23
FROM NIGHTCLUBS TO STADIUMS

In 2014, Dan Auerbach admitted: "We never thought we'd get to this level. We spent years watching so many other bands rise to the top, go right past us in a sports car while we're in a minivan. A year later, their sports car breaks down on the side of the road. And we're still going." When the Black Keys triumphantly returned to Northeastern Ohio for a sold-out gig at Quicken Loans Arena, Auerbach took a drive around the city of Cleveland. Reminiscing about the band's first concert at the Beachland Ballroom, he told *Rolling Stone*: "We got paid $10, and then for the second gig they didn't pay us anything."

Also that year, Auerbach produced an album for high-profile singer-songwriter, Lana Del Rey. They had met in New York City while Auerbach was mixing an album for Ray Lamontagne at Electric Lady Studios. A few days later, Auerbach spotted Del Rey in a nightclub, where they danced together and talked about music.

The following day, Del Rey played her songs for Auerbach. She stated at the time: "He gave me some confidence back. He listened to songs that were folk songs at the time, and he thought that maybe, with some revision, they could be more dynamic. I started to see a bigger picture. For me, if I don't have a concept it's not worth writing a whole album. I don't like it if there's no story." Auerbach recalled: "Her songs were so strong that I wanted to get my musicians in who I love and get my sound that I get here with her songs and that's it. I didn't want to mess it up. She sang live with a seven-piece band. That's the whole record – a seven-piece band with her singing live. It was crazy."

At Easy Eye Sound, the sessions were scheduled for just three-days but continued for several weeks. In the studio, the two headstrong musicians often clashed. Auerbach recalled: "With Lana, that was the first time I worked with anyone who had a lot of pressure from a label. She was under the gun, being questioned about money. It was hard. But I love the recordings we did, so it was worth it." In addition to producing about half of the album's tracks, Auerbach also contributed guitar, synthesizer and backing vocals. Released in June 2014, *Ultraviolence* was Del Rey's first number-one album. One reviewer wrote: "Producer Dan Auerbach, of the Black Keys, proves a good fit, giving the album a welcome lushness. Del Rey makes every song feel like a movie, and her voice has never been more commanding."

The Black Keys spent much of 2014 on the road. A reviewer

in Columbus, Ohio, wrote: "Playing against a backdrop designed to look like a Hollywood soundstage – dozens of stage lights formed a glowing metallic forest behind the musicians and assorted video screens projected what could have been termed raw footage – Auerbach and Co. dabbled in blues-rock, garage, psychedelia, glam, and... a breezy cover of the Kinks' 'Act Nice And Gentle.'"

In July of that year, the Black Keys were on the same bill as the Pretenders at a music festival in Suffolk, England. Carney recalled: "The Pretenders sounded awesome and [Chrissie Hynde] was super cool as usual, really nice. And then I posted [a] picture on Instagram and all the comments were 'Fatrick Carney,' and they were all fat jokes about me. So I went out and joined a gym because of Internet trolls."

*   *   *   *   *   *

The Black Keys knew they had finally made it to the big time when their hometown, minor league baseball team – the Akron Rubber Ducks – issued a bobblehead that featured the likenesses of Dan Auerbach and Patrick Carney. Carney wasn't completely happy with the figurine: "I like it, but I notice my pants and Dan's pants are pulled up pretty high on that bobblehead. I wouldn't wear my pants that high. I don't think I'd tuck in a baseball jersey either, but, whatever, it's cool.... I would've gone to the game but we were in France." The team would also issue bobbleheads of other Northeastern Ohio musical acts such as Devo, Chrissie Hynde and Joe Walsh.

*   *   *   *   *   *

In a battle of Midwestern blues-based rock duos, singer-guitarist Jack White of the White Stripes repeatedly accused the Black Keys of pirating the Detroit act's sound. In 2010, White went public with his beef in a *Rolling Stone* interview. However, Dan Auerbach insisted he was unaware of the White Stripes when he co-founded the Black Keys. Additionally, he insisted that he would have selected a different name for the duo had he known about White's band. Although the White Stripes would disband in 2011, the conflict continued to simmer.

The conflict intensified in 2012, when Auerbach was blocked from attending a musical performance that was staged at White's recording studio in Nashville, Third Man Records. When asked for additional details by *Rolling Stone* magazine, White simply confirmed that the incident occurred.

The beef continued in 2013, when White's emails to his ex-wife, Karen Elson, were publicized in the rock press. He again accused the Black Keys of ripping him off. The following year, White stated: "There are kids at school who dress like everybody else, because they don't know what to do, and there are musicians like that, too. I'll hear TV commercials where the music's ripping off sounds of mine, to the point I think it's me. Half the time, it's the Black Keys." However, Auerbach stated at the time: "I was pretty surprised by anything he said. I hardly knew the guy."

The conflict nearly turned ugly during a verbal confrontation on September 14, 2015, when Pat Carney was having a drink at the Cabin Down Below tavern in New York City. Afterward, Carney tweeted: "I've never met Jack White. Until last night. He came into a bar in NYC... A 40-year-old bully tried to fight a 35-year-old nerd. It might get loud but it might also get really sad and pathetic." White responded to the post with a statement to *Pitchfork*, denying that he was trying to start a fight.

Carney subsequently responded with a statement to the media: "I got into music because of people like him. The bully assholes who made me feel like nothing. Music was a collaborative and non-competitive thing. So, to get macho bullshit from within the musical community makes me angry and sad." Soon after, Carney and White spoke on the phone for a full hour and settled their dispute.

▶ CHAPTER 24

STEPPING BACK FROM THE KEYS

By the end of 2014, Dan Auerbach and Pat Carney were physically and emotionally drained from twelve-years of nonstop touring and recording, and were approaching a breaking point. After performing eighty concerts that year, they desperately wanted to take a break.

In January 2015, Carney was injured while bodysurfing on the Carribean island of St. Barths. He was hit by a massive wave and sent crashing into the ocean floor. Consequently, the Black Keys were forced to cancel a number of upcoming shows.

The mishap gave Auerbach the time to finish an album with his other band, the Arcs. Auerbach insisted at the time: "This is not a side-project; this is not a solo project. This is a real band." The Arcs also included Richard Swift, Nick Movshon, Homer Steinweiss and Leon Michels, who was previously a touring member of the Black Keys.

During this same period, Auerbach also produced an album

Chuck Auerbach, right, performing at Jilly's in Akron.

for his 66-year-old father, Chuck. The elder Auerbach had been writing songs for nearly fifteen-years up to that point. The sessions began at the Butcher Shoppe, a Nashville studio operated by John Prine and David Ferguson. Later, Chuck Auerbach added his vocals to the tracks at Easy Eye Sound.

Dan Auerbach said of his father: "He's ballsy, man. He set up the whole session. He called all the musicians, hired them, booked the studio, and he did it on a day that he knew I was available. So he said, 'Hey, I just wanted to let you know I'm doing this session if you feel like stopping by.' I couldn't say no. He knew I was home, and free, and I wasn't making a record."

Following the release of the album, *Remember Me*, Chuck Auerbach played a few hometown shows. Not surprisingly, when Auerbach and his band performed at Jilly's Music Room in downtown Akron, Pat Carney's father was seated in the audience.

Meanwhile, Carney struggled to recuperate from his injuries, which included a frozen shoulder. He was finally able to return to the stage in late-May for a limited number of concerts. In 2015, the Black Keys played just twenty-three shows, mostly over the summer at large European festivals. For their co-headlining slot at the prestigious Isle of Wight Festival, they opened with "Dead And Gone" and closed with "Little Black Submarines." A British reviewer wrote: "On Friday, the Black Keys offset a torrential downpour with a headline-worthy set of voodoo blues pop, northern soul, T-Rex glam and the sly bit of Rod Stewart bar-room boogie."

Still amazed by the level of his success, Auerbach told *Rolling Stone* magazine: "When we tell people that we can't believe we're headlining Coachella or whatever, we mean it. We are not the people that you would normally associate with being at the top of a pop food chain – generally to do that, you've got to have some star charisma."

In August 2015, the Black Keys took a much-deserved extended break. During this period, both men were able to pursue their own projects – mostly producing albums for other acts. Auerbach, in particular, wanted to spend some time away from the Black Keys. He explained: "We'd been caged up together for so long. When you're on tour, you're just up in each other's business, 24/7. So it's really healthy to have a little time apart after that kind of cohabitation." Carney also realized the duo needed a respite: "It was fun going on tour and getting to play concerts for so many people, but... at this point, we have children and the idea of putting a record out and being on the road for eight months and flying around the world seemed unrealistic." However, neither Auerbach nor Carney had expected their hiatus to last four-years.

*   *   *   *   *   *

In late-2015, Dan Auerbach's *other* group, the Arcs, released an album of original material – *Yours, Dreamily*. Auerbach explained: "We're absolutely record geeks and I think the Arcs' record is a kind of representation of all of our record collections." Saxophonist Leon Michels recalled: "There were like 40 songs recorded. We were just constantly making music. There was never that much pressure to record the record. We were just recording.... But there's like 30 songs that didn't make the record."

Backing the Arcs on the sessions was the New York-based all-female mariachi band, Flor de Toloache. Auerbach explained: "Leon [Michels] and I were in Mexico and wrote a couple of songs, and we thought it would be a supercool idea to have a mariachi band play on them.... And then they started playing, and they were so great. We just kept putting them on different songs. Then we asked if they could sing, and of course, they sang great."

The Arcs toured in support of their debut album, which peaked in the U.S. at a respectable number-twenty-seven on *Billboard's* sales chart. During the tour, Auerbach refused to play any Black Keys songs. He stated at the time: "We're still doing some figuring each other out. I'm onstage with eight people and everyone is listening, and I think the first few shows, we were all kind of too nervous. But once we started settling down, we started to get into a little bit of a 'thing.'" In November, Chrissie Hynde took the stage at an Arcs show in London and performed two songs – the 1960s oldie "Be My Baby" and a Pretenders track written by Ray Davies, "I Go To Sleep."

Also in 2015, Auerbach produced the album, *Tell Me I'm Pretty,* by Cage the Elephant. Auerbach recalled: "They approached me about producing the record and I'm not a modern rock kind of guy, it's not necessarily the kind of records I make. But Matt and Brad (Shultz) came up to my hotel room when we were in Chicago, had an acoustic guitar, and then I just thought they had some really great songs. Matt had stepped up his game in every way, so I agreed to do the record." Brad Shultz described the recording process: "We thought Dan was really good at putting parts in that would have an emotional depth or impact on a listener. It helped to see some little tricks that Dan uses to think out the track but still have some really great parts."

The album's first single, "Mess Around," was criticized in the music press for sounding too much like the Black Keys, with one reviewer complaining: "While I thoroughly enjoyed the song, something about it bothered me.... 'This isn't a Cage the Elephant song at all. It's a Black Keys song' I shouted at my radio." The project would earn a Grammy in the category of Best Rock Album.

In September 2015, Auerbach got married for the second time. His wife, Jen Goodall, was raised in England and Australia. The ceremony took place at their home in Nashville. Also that year, the namesake of the Black Keys – Akron artist Alfred McMoore – passed away at the age of 59.

*   *   *   *   *   *

In February 2015, Pat Carney first met Michelle Branch at a post-Grammy party in Los Angeles. At the time, Carney was separated from his second wife, Emily Ward, whom he would divorce the following January. A successful singer-songwriter, Branch first made waves in 2001 with her second album, *The Spirit Room*, which sold two-million copies and spawned three top-40 pop hits. However, she is best known for her 2002 collaboration with Santana – the top-10 hit, "The Game Of Love." Due to creative differences, Branch was eventually dropped by her label, Maverick Records.

Shortly after meeting Branch, Carney agreed to produce her next album. He stated at the time: "I tend to gravitate towards these David vs. Goliath projects; I always naturally side with an underdog – even with Michelle. When I agreed to help Michelle make the record it was because I really liked Michelle and wanted to get to know her, but also her struggle with trying to be heard, with being dropped by a record label which she had sold millions of records for. That really drew me in and made me want to help her." During the recording sessions in Los Angeles, the two musicians grew closer and began dating.

*   *   *   *   *   *

In April 2016, Pat Carney threw the ceremonial first pitch at the Cleveland Indians season opener as former player Sandy Alomar was positioned in the catcher's box. Carney said at the time: "I was nervous. I have been practicing, though. I dislocated and broke my shoulder last year and we had to

142

cancel some tours.... I am just happy that I kept the ball in the air. It wasn't over the plate, but it was in the air. It didn't bounce." Around this same time, Carney teamed with his uncle, Ralph Carney, to write the theme song for the Netflix animated series, *BoJack Horseman*.

That same year, the Black Keys were selected to induct Steve Miller into the Rock and Roll Hall of Fame. Auerbach recalled meeting Miller for the first time on the morning of the event: "He had no idea who we were. No idea. The first thing he told us was, 'I can't wait to get out of here.' He knew that we signed up to do this speech for him. And he made no effort to... even figure out who we were. I don't live in New York City. This is like three days out of my life flying from Nashville and leaving my kids at home."

At the induction ceremony, Auerbach and Carney took the stage and gave a five-minute speech honoring Miller. Carney later regretted one thing he said about Miller: "I wrote one line of our speech. It was the opening line.... It must've pissed him off. I didn't think about it. I said something like, 'There's been a lot of Millers from Milwaukee but only one of them wrote 'Fly Like An Eagle.' That's something a total shithead would say."

Shortly after the ceremony, an angry Miller viciously attacked the Rock Hall as well as the induction process. As expected, neither Auerbach nor Carney were happy about Miller's outburst. In a subsequent interview with *Billboard*, Miller tried to mend fences with the Black Keys: "I think their experience was as bad as mine. It shouldn't have happened, and if the Rock and Roll Hall of Fame would have had good enough manners to at least introduce us, we'd probably be friends. We have a lot in common.... I don't know them, and I don't have any bad feelings about them at all. I feel badly for them, because they've got to think, 'welcome to the Rock and Roll Hall of Fame, kid, here's how it works.'"

Additionally, Miller stated: "I wanted to ask Elton John to induct me, because Elton knows my music and loves my music and we're friends... But they said, 'no, the Black Keys are going to do it,' and I said, 'well, OK,' and they said 'there's no negotiation on any of it, that's the way we do it, that's the way we've always done it, that's the way it's gonna be. It's all gonna be a surprise; you're not gonna know what they're gonna say, you're not going to know anything about that.'"

CHAPTER 25

GLENN SCHWARTZ & CHRISSIE HYNDE

Also in 2016, Dan Auerbach paid homage to one of his early musical influences: "When I was 17, I'd go see Glenn Schwartz play every Thursday at Hoopples in Cleveland. He was the original guitar player on the James Gang – he's Joe Walsh's guitar hero, and he's a *badass*." Back in 2003, Auerbach hired Schwartz as the opening act for a number of Black Keys shows around Northeastern Ohio, including at the Lime Spider in Akron.

Schwartz had grown up listening to blues records, not a common activity in a middle-class suburb during the 1950s. But this was Northeastern Ohio, where deejay Alan Freed was playing music for black and white listeners alike. Drawn to rock and roll, Schwartz joined his first notable local band in the late-1950s, Frank Samson and the Wailers. Later, as a member of the Pilgrims – a British Invasion-style group – Schwartz scored a local hit with "Plymouth Rock." Drafted into the army in 1964, Schwartz was stationed in England, where he received some lessons from guitar virtuoso, Jeff Beck.

After returning to Cleveland in 1966, Schwartz yearned to restart his music career and was convinced to join an early version of the James Gang. Schwartz, who was significantly older than his bandmates, brought a new level of musical sophistication to the group's sound. He also garnered a reputation for his stage antics. *Scene* magazine reported: "Like Hendrix and the Who, Glenn wanted to give audiences a show that would leave them stunned. During a solo, Glenn would throw his legs over [bandmate Tom] Jeric's shoulders, then play guitar hanging upside down, as Jeric swung his torso. 'I'd bang his head against the stage,' says Jeric. 'He loved it when I drew blood.'"

In December 1967, Schwartz abruptly quit the James Gang and joined the Los Angeles-based rock band, Pacific Gas & Electric. He was replaced in the James Gang by his good friend, Joe Walsh. Returning to Cleveland in the early-1970s, Schwartz suffered from psychological problems and lived out of his car for a time. Despite encouragement and aid from the local music community, he was never able to again achieve any level of success outside of Ohio.

In February 2016, Auerbach brought Schwartz down to Easy Eye Sound in Nashville. Auerbach said of Schwartz: "He was my guitar hero growing up in Akron, and man, I just borrowed so much from him when I was starting, especially when I was starting the Black Keys.... I invited him to Nashville to record, and it was amazing." Auerbach described the sessions: "I brought Joe [Walsh] in... and it was so much fun just playing that raw rock and roll. I didn't realize how much it affected me until I got in that room with Glenn. I could hear all the licks I'd borrowed for the early Black Keys records. That was straight out of Glenn.... And *that* was the inspiration to make a new Black Keys record. It was kind of funny and totally unexpected, but very real. I felt it deeply – it was almost like going to church."

After spending a week in the studio, the trio staged a surprise performance at Robert's Western World in downtown Nashville. Backed by Auerbach's band, the Arcs, the three talented guitarists grinded out a number of blues songs during a 45-minute set, with Schwartz on both vocals and lead guitar.

Two-months later, on April 16, the Arcs appeared at the Coachella Festival in Indio, California. Near the close of their set, the band was joined by Walsh and Schwartz, who performed two songs – "Fear & Doom" and "Water Street." A year later, Schwartz passed away at the age of 78.

Later in 2016, Auerbach worked with Chrissie Hynde at Easy Eye Sound. Hynde recalled: "He's on such a roll that guy, and I was absolutely thrilled that he agreed to work with me." Up to this point, the two musicians had rarely crossed paths. Hynde explained: "I never met him in Akron – we both bailed out of that place years ago – although I did meet Dan's dad there once! But with Dan, I just like the guy. You can tell a lot about a musician by the way he holds his guitar – you can really tell if he gets his rock 'n' roll music. And Dan truly gets rock 'n' roll music.... Dan is half my age but he seems older than me! He sits in his studio surrounded by vintage studio equipment, old sculptures and Nudie Cohn suits, listening to crackly old records."

Meanwhile, Hynde was experiencing some health issues during this period: "I got there, it was in November, and I had

Chrissie Hynde, right, performing in Akron.

some disgusting respiratory thing. I couldn't cancel the session, because I don't cancel things as a policy unless I'm literally on death's doorstep. Which I pretty much was – I was on five medications."

The sessions proceeded as planned. Hynde recalled: "The first day we were in the studio, I didn't know any of the guys I was working with, but they must have been talking about what they did over the weekend with their wives and stuff. And I said, 'Ah, I go to the cinema alone. I live alone. I go to gigs alone. I do all that shit on my own.' Just in passing. And Dan pointed at me and he goes, 'Write a song about it!' And that's the song that came out. I hadn't actually had the foresight to write it on my own.... I owe that song really to him. Frankly, I wouldn't have thought it was a very interesting subject!" Hynde also revealed at the time: "All of my songs are always autobiographical, and I kind of wish they weren't.... I wish I was more of a storyteller, but I'm not."

The album was completed in just two-weeks. Hynde recalled: "I wrote most of these songs on my own, but Dan came up with wonderful textures and guitar riffs, to the point where he gets co-credit on some of them." With Auerbach at the mixing board, many of the tracks had a somewhat garage-rock feel.

Kenny Vaughan, who played guitar on the album, recalled: "Recording with Chrissie was great. She's easy to work with and very open to trying things out. She'd stand there and sing live with the band, and we'd all get shivers when that voice came through the speakers." The ailing Hynde played on only two tracks: "Gotta Wait" and "Chord Lord." In October 2016, *Alone* was released as a Pretenders album, not a solo work, despite the fact that Hynde was the only member of the group to appear on the project.

▶ CHAPTER 26
APART AND SOLO

In early-2017, Dan Auerbach began recording his second solo album. He admitted that the project could not have been made earlier in his career: "I felt like I had to wait my whole life to be able to make this record. The stars had to be aligned. For me, I'd never sat down with an acoustic guitar and tried to write a song with someone else, as they do in Nashville.... I had to make a conscious decision to stop touring altogether, to really focus. That was hard for me, because all I know is touring. To say no to that, is to say no to a lot of money."

For the sessions, Auerbach assembled a backing band that included a number of legendary Nashville-based musicians, including John Prine, Jerry Douglass, David Roe, Bobby Wood and Duane Eddy, who in 1988 had turned down George Harrison's invitation to join the original lineup of the Traveling Wilburys.

Auerbach described the album's songwriting process: "When I was growing up, we'd sit around in a circle and play guitar and sing bluegrass and blues songs. Now, I'm sitting in a circle with the guys who wrote many of those bluegrass and blues songs and we're writing together. Even though it was the first time I did it, something about it felt very natural." The musicians would write songs from Monday to Wednesday and then record from Thursday to Saturday. Auerbach described his state of mind at the time: "Sometimes I feel like I created my own *Field Of Dreams*. I am working with some of the greatest musicians that ever lived."

In June 2017, Auerbach released the completed album, *Waiting On A Song*, which he described as a "love letter" to Nashville. (Amazingly, the album was even issued in the 8-track format!) The first single, the jangly, pop-tinged, "Shine On Me," was a multi-format hit and topped *Billboard's* Adult-Alternative chart. The song featured Mark Knopfler of Dire Straits on rhythm guitar. Auerbach recalled: "That was a strange one because I still have yet to meet him. I cut 'Shine On Me' and as we were listening to playback, I was sitting at the console and I said out loud, 'This sounds like Mark Knopfler should be playing guitar on it.' So I had my manager reach out and ask him nicely. We sent the track, and two days later he sent back the song and it was exactly what the song needed. It was amazing. That describes this whole process; when the stars align and things happen between a song and a place... that's what this whole thing has been like."

Also in 2017, Auerbach teamed with Louisiana-born blues guitarist Robert Finley to record the soundtrack for the graphic novel, *Murder Ballads*. Auerbach subsequently produced Finley's solo album, *Goin' Platinum!* Finley recalled: "[Auerbach] put me in his studio with his session guys to woodshed. These guys were my heroes. They had played on my favorite records by Joe Tex and Aretha Franklin, many of the ones I heard coming out of that juke joint when I was a kid. It was like coming full circle.... You know, I am 63, and I'm looking round the room and I'm the youngest there and I'm overwhelmed by the experience in that room and when you got the best of the best pushing you, it's not hard to stay in your lane." (Auerbach and Finley would later reconvene for a second album in 2021.)

Meanwhile, Michelle Branch's album, *Hopeless Romantic*, was issued in April 2017. Three-months later, on her 34th birthday, she became engaged to Pat Carney. He revealed: "She changed my life. We started out friends who worked well together, and out of that fell in love. Neither of us saw it coming, and it's been wonderful." Enjoying his role as a producer, Carney would also work with Jessy Wilson, Calvin Johnson, Tennis and Dams of the West.

In December, Carney's uncle, Ralph, passed away at the age of 61. He suffered a fatal head injury at his home in Oregon. Over the years, Ralph Carney had frequently made guest appearances at Black Keys concerts. Pat Carney recalled: "Watching him make music was a spiritual thing.... I remember when my grandmother was dying in 1995 and I was 14 at the hospital and just getting into music. Ralph was there in the hospital and just pulled out a flute to play her a song. I had never heard something so profound in my life."

▶ CHAPTER 27
THE KEYS REUNITE

In the spring of 2018, Dan Auerbach revealed that he had recorded a "couple hundred" songs over the previous eighteen-months. Remaining devoted to his craft, he continued to spend a great deal of time at Easy Eye Sound. He admitted: "I was destined to do it. I can't do anything else, and I'm definitely doing what I'm supposed to do."

However, Auerbach wasn't making any music as a member of the Black Keys. His partner in the duo, Pat Carney, said at the time: "We're both just sort of homebodies and not that social when we're off the road, and this was obviously an unusually long break from touring. We actually had to make a point of meeting up for dinner once in a while, which is something we'd never really done before."

In September of that year, the Black Keys finally reunited in the studio. Carney explained the reasons for the long hiatus: "We had kind of just burned out by 2014, definitely by 2015.

155

I'd broken my shoulder in early-2015 and we had to cancel a bunch of dates. When we came back to finish a few dates we decided to not book any more shows and give ourselves some time off. Dan was going to go on tour with his band the Arcs, which led to him doing a solo tour and led to me doing a tour with Michelle [Branch]. One thing just kind of followed the other. That break we took, I think it saved our relationship, really. It proved to both of us that it's okay to slow things down. It's not a prison sentence; when we're excited about doing it we can do it, and if we need a break we can take a break."

Carney also pointed out: "Looking at some of our peers like Vampire Weekend or Arcade Fire, it's pretty normal for a band to take three and four years off, which is essentially what we did. It's unusual for us because we've never done it before." Nevertheless, he was concerned about the future of the Black Keys: "I knew we were going to make another record. The only thing that freaked me out was that the last show we played was in San Francisco and, man, every band breaks up in San Francisco." Carney was referencing the final concerts by the Sex Pistols, the Band and the Beatles.

Typically, before starting a new album, Auerbach and Carney would listen to a few dozen vinyl albums from the wall of records at Easy Eye Sound. That was not the case this time around. Auerbach recalled: "We didn't even talk about it. Honestly, we didn't listen to any music to get inspiration from anything. We got into the studio, made fun of each other for about 30 minutes, and then started playing. I had a microphone, and this is what came out. We were really flying by the seat of our pants." Additionally, Carney explained the importance of

156

self-producing the album: "We've only worked with one producer and that's Danger Mouse. He's one of my best friends. But, this time, it was important for Dan and I to go in there, just the two of us. We needed to work on our own communication."

In April 2019, Carney married Michelle Branch at the Marigny Opera House in New Orleans. The couple walked down the aisle to the Elvis Presley classic, "I Can't Help Falling In Love With You," which was performed by the Symphony Chorus of New Orleans.

In June, the Black Keys released their comeback album, *Let's Rock*. The cover featured an image of an electric chair. Auerbach revealed: "I was reading *The Tennessean*... and one of the headlines had 'Let's Rock' in quotations. They had just executed a prisoner... by electric chair. They asked him if he had any final words, and he said, 'Let's rock.' When we were thinking about album titles, it just kept coming back to my mind. Those were his last words and he said to them the day we were recording, and we had just made a rock and roll record. It just felt like a sign or something, like we were supposed to use it."

The album was more guitar-driven than the duo's previous efforts. Carney explained at the time: "We've both been playing a lot of electric guitar. Dan told me he basically stopped playing electric guitar for a while when he was producing a lot over the last couple years. Then he kind of rediscovered his guitar right before we started the record. That's why it sounds like a classic Keys record."

The album's first single, "Lo/Hi," topped the Alternative Rock chart. The song featured the backing vocals of Leisa Hans and Ashley Wilcoxson. Later, the album's third single, "Go," attracted some unexpected attention. The Black Keys' former rival, Jack White, praised the song in an online post: "More evidence that Nashville rock 'n' roll is alive and well. Congrats on the new music, @theblackkeys!"

The music video for "Go" mocked the duo's many detractors. The clip opens with Auerbach and Carney angrily sitting together on a therapist's couch, where they're admonished for refusing to speak to each other for five-years. Ordered to attend a new-age spiritual retreat, they remain hostile toward each other. However, after drinking a psychedelic potion, they both experience the same vision – a huge pile of money – and immediately decide to resolve their personal issues.

Around this time, the Black Keys agreed to perform a reunion show at the Woodstock 50 festival in August. However, they quickly backtracked. As Carney explained: "We realized that we didn't want our first show back to be in front of 150,000 people in a field without any control. We almost gave our agent a heart attack. We hadn't made any money in almost five-years and we got offered, like, $1.5 million. And we told him we don't want it. We only want to do stuff that actually is going to be enjoyable." It was the largest amount of money the group had ever been offered for a single performance.

Instead, the Black Keys hit the road for a tour in September. They were backed onstage by multi-instrumentalist Delicate Steve and brothers Andy and Zachary Gabbard of the Buffalo Killers. Modest Mouse was the opening act for most of the tour. Carney stated at the time: "It's a big step down from the 120 shows we did [for *El Camino*].... It's the only position I can think of where you're expected to go promote your record on, like, five different continents. This time... we're just going to stay here and ease back into the road."

Also that year, Carney joined forces with singer-guitarist John Petkovic of the Cleveland-based bands, Death of Samantha and Cobra Verde, to form Sad Planets. The group released the album, *Akron, Ohio*. Auerbach, meanwhile, produced the critically acclaimed album, *Walk Through Fire*, by British-born country/soul singer Yola Carter, which received four Grammy nominations. The project helped Auerbach to earn yet another Producer of the Year nomination.

Around this time, Auerbach's love of record collecting had evolved into a side gig. While touring, he occasionally stepped into nightclubs to work as a guest deejay with his own crate of soul and rock records. Eventually, Auerbach was joined by Carney at the events, which were promoted as "record hangs." At his first appearance, Carney played Devo's robotic version of the Rolling Stones classic, "(I Can't Get No) Satisfaction."

Meanwhile, Auerbach divorced for a second time when his marriage to Jen Goodall ended after four-years. The couple managed to keep the details of their breakup out of the press.

*   *   *   *   *   *

On March 5, 2020, the Black Keys announced a second leg of their Let's Rock tour, beginning with a July show at the White River Amphitheatre in Seattle. What no one realized at the time was that a worldwide pandemic would soon shut down the entire music industry. Consequently, the tour was cancelled.

During the lockdown, Auerbach spent his time producing

projects for singer-songwriter Yola Carter and blues guitarist Robert Finley, while Carney produced material for his wife and the garage band, Bass Of Death.

Auerbach and Carney never forgot the crucial mentoring they received from Sleater-Kinney and Beck during the early years of the Black Keys and returned the favor by helping a series of emerging acts.

Carney, meanwhile, also discovered a new hobby: "During the Covid year, I turned 40 and I took up the game of golf like every middle-aged man should do. I golfed with Alice [Cooper] and he was like 'Akron? You know, half of my band is from Akron.'"

▶ CHAPTER 28
TWENTY YEARS OF KEYS

On Dan Auerbach's 42nd birthday in 2021, the Black Keys released an album of cover songs, *Delta Kream*. The project was recorded in December 2019 after the completion of the first leg of the Let's Rock tour. Over two afternoons at Easy Eye Sound, the duo spent around ten-hours playing a number of North Mississippi-style blues songs. The sessions were unplanned.

Dan Auerbach recalled: "I called Pat up, and I didn't even know he was in town. And I said, 'What are you doing tomorrow?' and he cleared his schedule and he came over and we just jammed for the afternoon, just for fun... We weren't planning on making an album necessarily, but within a couple hours we had recorded nine songs. So after that I was like: we should just do a couple more in case we want to put it out."

Acknowledging his musical influences on the project, Carney stated at the time: "If it weren't for this music, I wouldn't have any of the things I have right now. I wouldn't have a band. I wouldn't be playing the drums. I wouldn't have done any of the things I've done. It starts there."

Auerbach and Carney were joined by a pair of Mississippi blues players – guitarist Kenny Brown and bassist Eric Deaton – both of whom had previously worked with Junior Kimbrough and R.L. Burnside. At the time, Brown and Deaton had just finished backing Louisiana bluesman Robert Finley on his solo album, *Sharecropper's Son*, which Auerbach had produced.

Delta Kream was well received by the early fans of the duo. Auerbach told a music journalist: "Yeah, there's probably zero commercial potential for this record, but it's important to put it out now while we still have people paying attention to our band – if only to showcase these guys who did so much to inspire us. I only heard about R.L. Burnside as a teenager because Jon Spencer made [an album] with R.L. If not for Spencer, who knows when I would have heard of R.L. Maybe we can do the same for some 16-year-old kids today." Amazingly, the album reached the top-10 on *Billboard's* sales chart.

The cover of the album featured a 1970 Oldsmobile Cutlass parked in front of a shuttered ice cream stand in Tunica, Mississippi. William Eggleston, the famed photographer who shot the photo, allowed the Black Keys to use the image for free. The album was highlighted by a cover of Junior Kimbrough's arrangement of the blues standard, "Crawling Kingsnake." The song's music video was filmed at the Blue Front Café, a juke joint in Bentonia, Mississippi, that is considered the oldest such venue in America. The album's release was tied to the Mississippi tourism board's campaign to promote a pair of new historical markers on the Mississippi Blues Trail featuring Kimbrough and Burnside. *Delta Kream* was later nominated for a Grammy in the category of Best Contemporary Blues Album.

* * * * * *

With the pandemic still raging, the Black Keys quietly celebrated their 20th anniversary in 2021. Around this time, Pat Carney recalled a conversation he had when first forming the duo, two-decades earlier: "Dan's dad asked me, 'Where do you think you guys could go?' I remember saying to him, 'I'll be really happy if we can play to 500 people,' which was the small room at the Agora in Cleveland. That would have been the peak for me."

Reflecting on the duo's hard-earned success, Auerbach stated: "We definitely made our name by hitting the road. And we hit the road when we were young, zigzagging all across North America and not making any money. For a while it felt like each tour we were starting over. There was this time, we felt there was no possibility we could keep doing it. It was a psychotic way of touring. We drove multiple vehicles into the ground. Because of that I have a hard time staying still these days. I get impatient."

Meanwhile, *The New York Times* asked the question: "Are the Black Keys still underdogs? They have sold more records than a lot of pop stars who are much more famous than they will ever be, but they're still another band from Akron, Ohio." And despite their multiple Grammy awards and sold-out arena tours, the duo had yet to score *one* top-40 hit on either the U.S. or U.K. pop charts.

Maintaining his hectic schedule during this period,

Auerbach produced Hank Williams Jr.'s 2022 album, *Rich White Honky Blues*. (The title was inspired by a phrase comedian Redd Fox uttered on an episode of the '70s sitcom, *Sanford And Son*.) The veteran country singer had always wanted to record a blues album and would tackle a number of classics by artists such as R.L. Burnside, Robert Johnson and Lightnin' Hopkins. Williams said at the time: "I got over there with... Dan [Auerbach], and it was just like pouring water out of a cup. It went pretty smooth and we knocked it out in two and a half days." One reviewer wrote: "Auerbach's biggest contribution may have been a determination not to round off any of the rough edges, and there are plenty."

Later, the Black Keys appeared at the 2022 VetsAid concert, which was staged in Columbus, Ohio. The duo's ten-song setlist began with "Howlin' For You" and closed with "Lonely Boy." The annual charity fundraiser – which was launched by Joe Walsh and emceed by Cleveland native Drew Carey – featured a number of other Ohio artists, including Nine Inch Nails, Dave Grohl, the Breeders and a reunited James Gang. Meanwhile, with their 25th high school reunions approaching, both members of the Black Keys announced they would not be attending.

▶ CHAPTER 29
PANDEMIC BLUES

With the pandemic waning and the concert industry slowly returning to normal, the Black Keys wanted to get back on the stage. When they were invited to headline the Pilgrimage Festival in nearby Franklin, Tennessee, as a last-minute replacement, they jumped on the opportunity. Before the concert, the duo decided to first play some smaller shows close to home, across the South.

In June 2021, the Black Keys began working on their next album. The project was recorded over a four-month period at Easy Eye Sound. Auerbach described the tracks: "Some of the songs are a little more pop-minded, thinking about it in terms of, 'How do we make something catchy.' We wanted to have some of those on the record. We also wanted to have some very raw improvisations. And I think we got a healthy mixture."

During the middle of the sessions, Billy Gibbons of ZZ Top – who was visiting Nashville – was invited to the studio. Auerbach and Carney had belatedly become fans of ZZ Top after listening to the group's first two albums. Auerbach recalled: "The whole Billy F. Gibbons thing – I texted him in the morning because I'd heard he was in town, and he showed up later that day and we just jammed together. All the collaborations on the record were just so easy, very nice."

However, Gibbons was planning to simply hang out and chat with Auerbach and Carney – not to play on the album. Auerbach recalled: "He didn't bring a guitar; he just had a bottle of wine. I handed him a guitar [previously owned by Fred McDowell], plugged it right into the amp, turned it all the way up and we were off for the races. We played for two-and-a-half-hours, just improvising, having fun, and then he took off and we had the song." Gibbons' contributions were featured on the track, "Good Love." Carney explained: "That's us playing... with no rehearsal and riding that whole groove on the spot. That's kind of the essence of our band, making something and not seeking perfection, not rehearsing it, not stewing over a riff for weeks or months."

On another track, "Happiness," Auerbach played a guitar once owned by blues legend, Hound Dog Taylor. Auerbach recalled: "I bought it off of Bruce Iglauer, who founded Alligator Records... and I use it all the time. It's a big, old Japanese guitar with four pickups that is just wild."

In May 2022, the Black Keys released their eleventh studio album, *Dropout Boogie*. The title was taken from a 1967 song by one of the duo's early influences, experimental blues-rocker Captain Beefheart. It was the duo's sixth top-10 album in a row. *Classic Rock* magazine named it the number-forty-seven best album of the year, calling it "a refreshing dash of bubblegum soul and pop."

On the album's cover and in the music video for the first single, "Wild Child," the members of the Black Keys imagined the jobs they might have if not for their successful music careers. Carney explained at the time: "Dan's daughter's in high school and my stepdaughter is in high school. We were talking about our high school experience and how insane it was – like kids getting thrown through trophy cases and absolute madness – versus what our kids are experiencing. And so we wanted to do a video that was not mocking today's high school students, but maybe trying to show what kind of trouble they could get into. I was like, 'Yeah, we can play the teacher and the guidance counselor!' and Dan's like, 'No, man. We dropped out of school. We'd have to be the janitor and the cook.'" The video was filmed at a high school near Nashville.

"Wild Child" was co-written by Auerbach, Carney, Greg Cartwright of the group Reigning Sound and songwriter-producer Angelo Petraglia. Cartwright recalled: "I've never experienced anything like that in my life! Usually you write a song and there's weeks or months in between that moment of inspiration and when it gets laid down on tape. But Dan loves the idea of catching something when it's fresh. There's some kind of magic there that you might lose if you continue to play and record it. And I think that's what makes the Black Keys work... There's not a lot of production going on, and not a lot of adjusting it after the fact. It is what it is." Cartwright also co-wrote the second single, "It Ain't Over," which opens with a riff from a vintage Optigan keyboard.

The success of the collaborations inspired the members of the Black Keys to repeat the formula on their next album, which featured of a number of well-known guest songwriters.

There were two legendary artists that Auerbach had hoped to work with sometime in the future – Van Morrison and Bob Dylan. However, Auerbach admitted: "Sometimes I think that would be fun, but most of the time I think, naaah, I probably shouldn't."

*   *   *   *   *   *

The Black Keys began 2023 by headlining the pre-game festivities at Super Bowl LVII in Glendale, Arizona. Later that month, they were nominated for two Grammys – in the categories of Best Rock Album and Best Rock Performance – but lost to Ozzy Osbourne and Brandi Carlile. At the ceremony, Pat Carney was joined by his wife, Michelle Branch, as he walked down the red carpet. Around this time, Auerbach's group, the Arcs, released their second album, *Electrophonic Chronic*.

Additionally, Auerbach released the compilation album, *Tell Everybody! 21st Century Juke Joint Blues From Easy Eye Sound*. The project included ten tracks by a variety of blues artists, including Gabe Carter, Robert Finley and Nat Myers. One of the tracks, "Daughter Of Zion" by Glenn Schwartz, featured the musical backing of Joe Walsh and the Arcs. The song was recorded shortly before Schwartz's passing in 2018.

Later that year at Easy Eye Sound, the Black Keys collaborated with their early supporter, singer-songwriter Beck. From the informal sessions, Auerbach and Carney began assembling an album of duets with a wide variety of well-known artists, including Noel Gallagher, formerly of Oasis.

Amazingly, the Black Keys were still at the top of their

168

game, although both members had clearly aged. Carney, in particular, now sported distinguished streaks of gray in his beard and on both sides of his head. Assessing his life and prioritizing his responsibilities, Carney admitted: "I have two little kids and that's what occupies my bandwidth. I'm happy to do the band stuff. Ten years ago, I would get so stressed out with work and the band and just the pressure. And now I'm like, what was wrong with me? Nothing compares to having to wrangle a toddler." However, Auerbach admitted: "We're both just totally addicted to recording even now. I don't know what it is. But we get such a high off getting in there and creating something out of nothing, pulling songs out of thin air. It's like this magic trick we learned to do when we were 16 and we never stopped. We never got tired of the trick."

▶ CLOSING TIME

In 2022, a full twenty-years after the release of the Black Keys' debut album, *The Big Come Up*, Dan Auerbach admitted: "We were just flying by the seat of our pants. We were shocked when we got a record deal. And we've been constantly shocked the whole 20 years we've been a band, really."

However, as of 2023, the Black Keys never reached *Billboard's* top-40. Their best-known song, "Lonely Boy," made it to just #64 on the chart. The same was true in Britain, where pop radio also ignored the duo. On the other hand, the Black Keys placed seventeen tracks on *Billboard's* rock chart in their first twenty years. During the same period, they reached the top-10 of *Billboard's* album chart a total of six times. Despite strong album sales, lucrative arena tours and multiple Grammy wins, the Black Keys have earned limited respect in mainstream popular music and are still viewed as an outsider act.

Both members of the duo continue to celebrate their hometown in Ohio despite relocating to Nashville. Pat Carney admitted: "I mean, Akron's always home, you know? You'll never know a place like your hometown." Likewise, Auerbach insisted: "Well, we will always be from Ohio, and that's always gonna be a humongous part of who we are and what we are about. That sort of working-class town, small town. If you want to do something you gotta do it yourself.... [The DIY thing] is how we did it. That's how we started. I think, for a long time, living there we kind of defined ourselves as an underdog type of band in an underdog type of city."

Remarkably, Auerbach and Carney were still able to maintain their close comradery as well as their creative relationship in the studio, more than two-decades after they crafted their first album in a dingy Akron basement. Carney revealed: "We're both very, very appreciative of what we've accomplished, and not just career goals but maintaining the relationship. It's taken a lot of work to maintain our friendship and get everything to where it needs to be. Anytime you spend a lot of time going from the bottom to the top, and then settling down wherever it is in the middle, that's a wild ride. Most bands don't make it through it, and when they do, a lot of times they hate each other or they turn into complete freaks." Additionally, Carney joked: "I think our relationship would be best described as a mixture between Patty and Selma Bouvier from *The Simpsons* and Erik Estrada and that other dude [Larry Wilcox] from *CHiPs*. We take turns playing each role."

▶ BIBLIOGRAPHY

1. Abram, Malcolm X. (2003, March 16). Duo Black Keys rock Texas fans. *The Akron Beacon Journal.*
2. Appleford, Steve. (2023, March 10). Dan Auerbach's vinyl obsessions and the return of the Arcs [video]. *The Los Angeles Times.*
3. Carney, Jim. (2016, November 13). Catching up with... *The Akron Beacon Journal.*
4. Catchpole, Chris. (2023, April). Let's shop. *Record Collector.*
5. Contrera, Jessica. (2014, September 26). Fame leaves Black Keys drummer without his pants. *The Washington Post.*
6. Doyle, Patrick. (2014, August 11). The dark days behind the Black Keys' best album yet. *Rolling Stone.*
7. Doyle, Tom. (2014, November). The Black Keys: Pat Carney & Dan Auerbach. *Sound on Sound.*
8. Eels, Josh. (2010, May 27). Two against nature. *Rolling Stone.*
9. Faris, Mark. (1984, January 15). Rubber City talent shines in spotlight. *The Akron Beacon Journal.*
10. Fricke, David. (2020). The Black Keys: *Brothers* [liner notes]. Nonesuch Records.
11. Graff, Gary. (2020, June 29). Q&A with the Black Keys. *Music Connection.*
12. "Harmonious." (1976, June 19). *The Akron Beacon Journal.*
13. Levine, Nick. (2022, May 13). Soundtrack of my life: The Black Keys' Patrick Carney. *NME* [online].
14. Lynskey, Dorian. (2010, September). Blues explosion! *Spin.*
15. Lynskey, Dorian. (2014, June). To infinity and beyond. *Mojo.*
16. O'Connor, Clint. (2002, December 27). Critics' favorite turns into headliner, gets Fat record deal. *The Cleveland Plain Dealer.*
17. Meeker, Ward. (2017, August). Dan Auerbach: Nashville collaborative. *Vintage Guitar.*
18. Niesel, Jeff. (2003, December 24). Akron's Black Keys cap a stellar year with a New Year's Eve show. *The Cleveland Free Times.*
19. Parkey, Victoria. (2023, January 20). Nine songs: Dan Auerbach. *The Line of the Best Fit* [online].
20. Poulsen, Andrew. (2016). Akron's audio alchemist. In Jason Segedy (Ed.) *The Akron Anthology.* Cleveland: Belt Publishing.
21. Prufer, Jason. (2019). *Small Town, Big Music: The Outsized Influence of Kent, Ohio, on the History of Rock and Roll.* Kent, OH: Kent State University Press.
22. Purcell, Andrew. (2010, July 9). 'It's ridiculous to say that we play the blues.' *The Independent.*
23. Runtagh, Jordan. (2017, June 6). Dan Auerbach talks going to the musical wellspring for 'Waiting on a Song,' and his recording 'addiction.' *People* [online].
24. Simons, Dave. (2011, August). Mark Neill: Recording the Black Keys at Muscle Shoals. *Sound on Sound.*
25. Smith, William Michael. (2015, May 12). Ohio bluesman Patrick Sweany's Black Keys connection. *HoustonPress* [online].
26. Stansberry Matt. (1996, October 17). Bands begin European tour. *The Daily Kent Stater.*
27. Talevski, Nick. (2009). *Hang on Sloopy: The History of Rock and Roll in Ohio.* Green, OH: Guardian Express Media.
28. Tatangelo, Wade. (2005, May 6). Paint it black: The Black Keys play heavy blues and dig Devo. *The Bradenton (Florida) Herald.*
29. "The Black Keys' front man Dan Auerbach worked with legends for new solo album." (2017, June 3). *CBS Mornings* (CBS).
30. Warwick, Neil; Kutner Jon; & Brown Tony. (2004). *The Complete Book of the British Charts, 3rd ed.* London: Omnibus Press.

31. Whitburn, Joel. (2008). *Rock Tracks 1981-2008*. Menomonee Falls, WI: Record Research.
32. Whitburn, Joel. (2018). *Top Pop Albums 1955-2016*. Menomonee Falls, WI: Record Research.
33. Whitburn, Joel. (2019). *Top Pop Singles 1955-2018*. Menomonee Falls, WI: Record Research.
34. White, Caitlin. (2016, August 12). Dad interrupted: Chuck Auerbach on his debut album, first-ever performance, and famous son. *Stereogum* [online].

▶ NOTES

INTRODUCTION:
1. "Employment in Akron rubber companies..." ~ Musarra, Russ. (2000, February). The Akron centesequinary celebration. *Northern Ohio Live.*
2. "One of my clearest memories..." ~ Warner, Brad. (2007). *Sit Down and Shut Up.* Novato, CA: New World Library.
3. "If you went high up..." ~ James, LeBron; & Bissinger, Buzz. (2009). *Shooting Stars.* New York: Penguin.
4. "It's kind of a strange..." ~ Uitti, Jacob. (2022, May 11). The Black Keys: Brothers in arms. American Songwriter.
5. "I think it was all..." ~ Guarino, Mark. (2006, October). Blues brothers. *Harp.*
6. "Dan and me grew up..." ~ Gafkjen, Alysse, (2021, July). Preachin' the blues. *Mojo.*
7. "Akron had the perfect recipe..." ~ Corona, Alessandro. (2022, August 30). Black Keys drummer gives shoutout to Shake It Records, Southgate House. *The Cincinnati Enquirer.*

CHAPTER 1:
1. "Patrick Carney, 5, in stonewashed..." ~ Cardwell, Jewell. (1985, August 4). 1-2-3, back-to-school shopping can be E-Z. *The Akron Beacon Journal.*
2. "We would go spend the..." ~ Crane, Larry. (2020, April/May). Patrick Carney of the Black Keys. *Tape Op.*
3. "When I was about seven..." ~ Crane, Larry. (2020, April/May). Patrick Carney of the Black Keys. *Tape Op.*
4. "My father moved into Dan's..." ~ Abdurraqib, Hanif. (2021, May 26). Are the Black Keys still underdogs? *The New York Times Magazine.*
5. "My dad was like, 'This..." ~ "Pat Carney: Black Keys beat." (2023, July). *Mojo.*
6. "Fit in a little bit..." ~ Price, Mark J. (2021, May 14). Informal sessions in late-2019 after completing an album for Louisiana singer-songwriter Robert Finley. *The Akron Beacon Journal.*
7. "By the time I was..." ~ Crane, Larry. (2020, April/May). Patrick Carney of the Black Keys. *Tape Op.*
8. "I just wanted to see..." ~ Carney, Jim. (2016, November 13). Catching up with... *The Akron Beacon Journal.*
9. "I wasn't very good at..." ~ Usinger, Mike. (2006, September-October). Modern primitives: The Black Keys insist on doing it themselves, thank you. *No Depression.*
10. "When I was 15, I..." ~ Crane, Larry. (2020, April/May). Patrick Carney of the Black Keys. *Tape Op.*
11. "I was obsessed with the..." ~ Hirsh, Marc. (2019, October 11). The beat goes on for the Black Keys' Patrick Carney. *The Boston Globe.*
12. "When I was 16, I..." ~ Petkovic, John. (2017, December 18). Ralph Carney, renowned Akron native musician. *The Cleveland Plain Dealer.*

CHAPTER 2:
1. "It was totally great. I..." ~ Guarino, Mark. (2006, October). Blues brothers. *Harp.*
2. "I was 16, but I..." ~ Deusner, Stephen. (2022, June). The Black Keys: Keys to the highway. *Uncut.*
3. "I really enjoyed high school..." ~ Daniell, Mark. (2022, May 14). The Black Keys get loose and forge a new path on 'Dropout Boogie.' *The Toronto Sun.*
4. "were listening to Yo La..." ~ Prufer, Jason. (2019). *Small Town, Big Music: The Outsized*

Influence of Kent, Ohio, on the History of Rock and Roll. Kent, OH: Kent State University Press.
5. "Pat must of booked these..." ~ Prufer, Jason. (2019). *Small Town, Big Music: The Outsized Influence of Kent, Ohio, on the History of Rock and Roll.* Kent, OH: Kent State University Press.
6. "First Jermaine [Blair] disappeared, and..." ~ Prufer, Jason. (2019). *Small Town, Big Music: The Outsized Influence of Kent, Ohio, on the History of Rock and Roll.* Kent, OH: Kent State University Press.
7. "draw the turtle" ~ Guarino, Mark. (2006, October). Blues brothers. *Harp.*

CHAPTER 3:
1. "I was getting straight A's..." ~ Mervis, Scott. (2009, June 4). Persistent approach opens doors for Black Keys. *The Pittsburgh Post-Gazette.*
2. "Her entire family was murdered..." ~ Simpson, Dave. (2011, December 1). 'We've put in more hours than anyone:' The Black Keys interviewed. *The Guardian.*
3. "Ever since I was a..." ~ Hiatt, Brian. (2012, January 19). The rise of the Black Keys: How two Rust Belt refugees became an arena-size, super-charged stomp machine. *Rolling Stone.*
4. "was like the outcast on..." ~ Perry, Andrew. (2017, August). The *Mojo* interview. *Mojo.*
5. "My dad was an antique..." ~ Christensen, Thor. (2022, October 13). The Black Keys' Dan Auerbach says the blues are alive and well. *The Dallas Morning News.*
6. "My dad did antique shows..." ~ Uhelszki, Jaan. (2018, May). Dan Auerbach: "I don't think I'm that much of a control freak any more..." *Uncut.*
7. "Nobody listens to music louder..." ~ Si Perna, Alan. (2014, September). Black & Blue. *Guitar World.*
8. "He'd blast out the Stones..." ~ Perry, Andrew. (2017, August). The *Mojo* interview. *Mojo.*

CHAPTER 4:
1 "It was eye opening, wild..." ~ Bonner, Michael. (2015, October). An audience with... Dan Auerbach. *Uncut.*
2. "When I was teaching myself..." ~ Moeller, Sean. (2003, October 30). Shortlist nod puts Black keys on fast track. *The (Davenport, IA) Quad-City Times.*
3. "There were more people listening..." ~ Herrera, Monica. (2009, November 28). Blak is the new roc. *Billboard.*
4. "I didn't really have much..." ~ Si Perna, Alan. (2014, September). Black & Blue. *Guitar World.*
5. "I've been playing guitar seriously..." ~ Kick, Richard. (1985, April. Red red Quine. *Zig Zag.*
6. "I think Quine was the..." ~ Hell, Richard. (2013). *I Dreamed I Was a Very Clean Tramp.* New York: Ecco.
7. "Quine got me playing guitar..." ~ Garbarini, Vic. (1986, July). Lou Reed: Waiting for the muse. *Musician.*
8. "My mom got me a..." ~ Male, Andrew. (2011, June). Exiles on Main Street. *Mojo.*
9. "He taught me how to..." ~ "Headliners: Dan Auerbach." (2009, October 28). *Columbus Alive!*
10. "The guy at the store..." ~ Parks, Andrew. (2005, January/February). My city was gone. *Magnet.*
11. "He lived in NYC and..." ~ Bonner, Michael. (2015, October). An audience with... Dan Auerbach. *Uncut.*
12. "The first time I heard..." ~ Drozdowski, Ted. (2021, Fall). The Black Keys Honoring North Mississippi. *Blues Music Magazine.*
13. "I didn't even like Chicago..." ~ Chinen, Nate. (2009, June 4). Dan Auerbach shows a different side. *The San Diego Union-Tribune.*
14. "I loved the sounds all..." ~ Hodgkinson, Will. (2006). *Guitar Man: A Six-String Odyssey.* London: Bloomsbury.
15. "I used to get videos ..." ~ Saufley, Charles. (2010, August). Future blues: The Black Keys' Dan Auerbach. *Premier Guitar.*

16. "If you watch them enough..." ~ Hodgkinson, Will. (2006). *Guitar Man: A Six-String Odyssey*. London: Bloomsbury.

CHAPTER 5:
1. "It reminded me of southern..." ~ Barton, Laura. (2021, May 16). Blues brothers. *The Independent*.
2. "Outside, the joint looked as..." ~ Cosyns, Simon. (2021, May 21). The Black Keys. *The Sun / Something For The Weekend*.
3 "We met his son Kinny..." ~ Graff, Gary. (2021, May 17). Akron-born Black Keys pay tribute to Mississippi Hill Country blues roots in new album, 'Delta Kream.' *The Cleveland Plain Dealer*.
4. "It was amazing. I got..." ~ Graff, Gary. (2021, May 17). Akron-born Black Keys pay tribute to Mississippi Hill Country blues roots in new album, 'Delta Kream.' *The Cleveland Plain Dealer*.
5. "Auerbach, needing to see more..." ~ Abdurraqib, Hanif. (2021, May 26). Are the Black Keys still underdogs? *The New York Times Magazine*.
6. "It was just like in..." ~ Abdurraqib, Hanif. (2021, May 26). Are the Black Keys still underdogs? *The New York Times Magazine*.
7. "I drove down to Mississippi..." ~ Relic, Peter. (2003, no. 4). On the road with the Black Keys and Sleater-Kinney. *Arthur*.
8. "hung out with more of..." ~ Tatangelo, Wade. (2005, May 6). Paint it black: The Black Keys play heavy blues and dig Devo. *The Bradenton (Florida) Herald*.
9. "We were in different grades..." ~ Uitti, Jacob. (2022, May 11). The Black Keys: Brothers in arms. *American Songwriter*.
10. "We both had the same..." ~ Nickoloff, Annie. (2022, July 27). The Black Keys' Dan Auerbach went from Blossom Music Center parking attendant to headliner (Q&A). *The Cleveland Plain Dealer*.

CHAPTER 6:
1. "Worst decision of my life..." ~ Guarino, Mark. (2006, October). Blues brothers. *Harp*.
2. "I was exposed to things..." ~ Vozick-Levinson, Simon. (2015, September 10). Q&A: Dan Auerbach. *Rolling Stone*.
3. "But I did hear the music..." ~ Christensen, Thor. (2022, October 13). The Black Keys' Dan Auerbach says the blues are alive and well. *The Dallas Morning News*.
4. "The first time I ever..." ~ Relic, Peter. (2003, no. 4). On the road with the Black Keys and Sleater-Kinney. *Arthur*.
5. "My dad told me that..." ~ Leahey, Andrew. (2011, November/December). The Black Keys: Brothers in arms. *American Songwriter*.
6. "Whatever the club needed I..." ~ Si Perna, Alan. (2014, September). Black & Blue. *Guitar World*.
7. "People weren't even listening at..." ~ Parks, Andrew. (2005, January/February). My city was gone. *Magnet*.
8. "[My father was] pushing me..." ~ Simmons, Sylvie. (2008, May). In from the cold. *Mojo*.
9. "I was actually making pretty..." ~ Si Perna, Alan. (2014, September). Black & Blue. *Guitar World*.
10. "[Auerbach] was great, he could..." ~ Abram, Malcolm X. (2012, March 20). How Black Keys have come up big. *The Akron Beacon Journal*.

CHAPTER 7:
1. "His name was Steve and..." ~ Usinger, Mike. (2006, September-October). Modern primitives: The Black Keys insist on doing it themselves, thank you. *No Depression*.
2. "Me and Dan had jammed..." ~ Cooper, Leonie. (2022, May 14). 'Technically, everything's wrong with it:' An oral history of the Black Keys' debut album at 20. *The Independent*.

3. "I had a summer off..." ~ Crane, Larry. (2020, April/May). Patrick Carney of the Black Keys. *Tape Op.*
4. "I didn't know how to..." ~ Cooper, Leonie. (2022, May 14). 'Technically, everything's wrong with it:' An oral history of the Black Keys' debut album at 20. *The Independent.*
5. "It was immediate, we could..." ~ Hiatt, Brian. (2012, January 19). The rise of the Black Keys: How two Rust Belt refugees became an arena-size, super-charged stomp machine. *Rolling Stone.*
6. "If it hadn't been for..." ~ Eels, Josh. (2010, May 27). Two against nature. *Rolling Stone.*
7. "We auditioned a couple people..." ~ Uhelszki, Jaan. (2014, July/August). The Black Keys: Chart-topping blues. *Relix.*

CHAPTER 8:
1. "There's something about Akron. It's..." ~ Bonner, Michael. (2015, October). An audience with... Dan Auerbach. *Uncut.*
2. "miserable and directionless" ~ Downing, Andy. (2019, October). Getting out of debt with Black Keys drummer Patrick Carney. *Columbus Monthly.*
3. "When I told my dad and..." ~ Daniell, Mark. (2022, May 14). The Black Keys get loose and forge a new path on 'Dropout Boogie.' *The Toronto Sun.*
4. "There was no plan B..." ~ Daniell, Mark. (2019, October 6). Back in black: Patrick Carney talks Black Keys comeback, realizing his rock dreams and why he always gets to choose the first and last song at every show they play. *The Toronto Sun.*
5. "A black key [on a piano]..." ~ Oldham, Tom. (2014, June). To infinity and beyond. *Mojo.*
6. "[McMoore] lived in a group..." ~ Usinger, Mike. (2006, September-October). Modern primitives: The Black Keys insist on doing it themselves, thank you. *No Depression.*
7. "I basically lived in a..." ~ Cooper, Leonie. (2022, May 14). 'Technically, everything's wrong with it:' An oral history of the Black Keys' debut album at 20. *The Independent.*
8. "I remember having to pick..." ~ Olivier, Bobby. (2022, April 25). After feeling 'Tense,' the Black Keys shake things up with new management & fresh songwriting process for 11th album. *Billboard.*
9. "We were shocked when we..." ~ Paulson, Dave. (2021, May 17). Interview: The Black Keys rediscover their blues roots, 20 years later. The *Tennessean.*

CHAPTER 9:
1. "I mean, I would say technically..." ~ Doyle, Tom. (2014, November). The Black Keys: Pat Carney & Dan Auerbach. *Sound on Sound.*
2. "My dad was so stressed..." ~ Cooper, Leonie. (2022, May 14). 'Technically, everything's wrong with it:' An oral history of the Black Keys' debut album at 20. *The Independent.*
3. "Despite their youth, you'd swear..." ~ Matheson, Emmet. (2002, December 26). Putting a rap on 2002. *The Regina Leader-Post.*
4. "I remember the day we..." ~ Clark, Eric. (2004, September 4). No stripes. The Black keys makes a name for itself. *The (Cedar Rapids, IA) Gazette.*
5. "We're like, 'No problem, we..." ~ Hall, Kristin. (2022, May 15). The Black Keys: Raw, fast and loose: Two decades ago at their first show together, the Black Keys played so fast they ran out of songs before their set ended. *The Roanoke Times.*
6. "I thought I was going..." ~ Abram, Malcolm X. (2006, June 24). Presenting Pat Carney – on guitar. *The Akron Beacon Journal.*
7. "They didn't have that garage..." ~ Yarborough, Chuck. (2013, February 11). Black Keys' 2013 Grammy wins attributed to hard work and Akron roots. *The Cleveland Plain Dealer.*
8. "I remember Pat's drum kit..." ~ Riemenschneider, Chris. (2012, May 13). A new arena for the Black Keys. *The Minneapolis Star Tribune.*
9. "pounds the drums harder than..." ~ Soeder, John. (2004, October 11). Akron-based duo doesn't

disappoint sold-out crowd. *The Cleveland Plain Dealer.*
10. "At first, we had to..." ~ Jacobs, Justin. (2008, August 7). The Black Keys get a Gnarly makeover. *The Pittsburgh Post-Gazette.*
11. "In Seattle, people were singing..." ~ O'Connor, Clint. (2002, December 27). Critics' favorite turns into headliner, gets Fat record deal. *The Cleveland Plain Dealer.*
12. "We played the next night at..." ~ Perry, Andrew. (2017, August). The *Mojo* interview. *Mojo.*
13. "a killer, bluesy Midwest two-piece..." ~ Relic, Peter. (2002, October 17). The Black Keys: *The Big Come Up. Rolling Stone.*
14. "The Black Keys aren't all..." ~ Mervis, Scott. (2003, June 6). The basement blues of the Black Keys. *The Pittsburgh Post-Gazette.*
15. "When we started out, we..." ~ Leslie, Jimmy. (2003, November). Fuzz freak: The Black Keys' Dan Auerbach on the majesty of muck. *Guitar Player.*
16. "You won't find the White..." ~ Usinger, Mike. (2006, September-October). Modern primitives: The Black Keys insist on doing it themselves, thank you. *No Depression.*

CHAPTER 10:
1. "We like challenges. When we..." ~ Uhelszki, Jaan. (2018, May). Dan Auerbach: "I don't think I'm that much of a control freak any more..." *Uncut.*
2. "We used to drive nine..." ~ Uhelszki, Jaan. (2019, July). Brothers gonna work it out. *Uncut.*
3. "Akron Duo Seems on Verge..." ~ Abram, Malcolm X. (October 24, 2002). Akron duo seems on verge of the big time. *The Akron Beacon Journal.*
4. "I actually had anxiety issues..." ~ White, Ryan. (2014, October 30). The Black Keys tour hits Sacramento on Tuesday. *The Sacramento Bee.*
5. "I'm nervous about messing up..." ~ Abram, Malcolm X. (October 24, 2002). Akron duo seems on verge of the big time. *The Akron Beacon Journal.*
6. "For two middle-class kids..." ~ Thomson, Graeme. (2012, March). How the Black Keys rose without a trace. *The Word.*
7. "They looked so young, young.." ~ Abdurraqib, Hanif. (2021, May 26). Are the Black Keys still underdogs? *The New York Times Magazine.*
8. "Within two hours, they're negotiating..." ~ Abdurraqib, Hanif. (2021, May 26). Are the Black Keys still underdogs? *The New York Times Magazine.*
9. "We were talking to some..." ~ "Album by album." (2013, January). *Uncut.*
10. "We were nervous to sign..." ~ Usinger, Mike. (2006, September-October). Modern primitives: The Black Keys insist on doing it themselves, thank you. *No Depression.*
11. "It's funny because we originally..." ~ Derdeyn, Stuart. (2022, September 27). Q&A: Black Keys' Dan Auerbach not singing the blues on new album Dropout Boogie. *The Vancouver Sun.*
12. "taught us a lot about..." ~ Mapes, Jillian. (2012, January 14). Tightened up. *Billboard.*

CHAPTER 11:
1. "We wanted this thing to..." ~ Tunis, Walter. (2004, March 19). Mississippi by way of Ohio. *The St. Joseph News-Press.*
2. "We always thought of this..." ~ Uhelszki, Jaan. (2018, May). Dan Auerbach: "I don't think I'm that much of a control freak any more..." *Uncut.*
3. "Everywhere we go, we let..." ~ Niesel, Jeff. (2004, October 6). Akron city limits. *The Cleveland Free Times.*
4. "The Black Keys got the..." ~ Danton, Eric R. (2003, February 15). Sleater-Kinney thrills its devotees. *The Hartford Courant.*
5. "We feel lucky. At least..." ~ Soeder, John. (2003, March 17). Akron blues-rockers impress audience at festival in Texas. *The Cleveland Plain Dealer.*
6. "Another band building momentum at..." ~ Gamboa, Glenn. (2003, March 17). In Austin, the

sounds serve as a barometer. *(New York) Newsday.*

7. "We're trying not to let..." ~ Soeder, John. (2003, March 17). Akron blues-rockers impress audience at festival in Texas. *The Cleveland Plain Dealer.*

8. "After this record came out..." ~ "Album by album." (2013, January). *Uncut.*

9. "We were getting weird phone..." ~ Niesel, Jeff. (2003, December 24). Akron's Black Keys cap a stellar year with a New Year's Eve show. *The Cleveland Free Times.*

10. "I remember the first time..." ~ Heldenfels, Rich. (2011, February 13). TV helps Black keys raise music profile. *The Akron Beacon Journal.*

11. "This whole year's been shocking..." ~ Moeller, Sean. (2003, October 30). Shortlist nod puts Black keys on fast track. *The (Davenport, IA) Quad-City Times.*

12. "We always feel like the..." ~ Niesel, Jeff. (2004, October 6). Akron city limits. *The Cleveland Free Times.*

CHAPTER 12:

1. "The rubber factory was a..." ~ Sculley, Alan. (2006, November 23). Black Keys keep live show interesting. *The (Madison, WI) Capital Times.*

2. "I had a ham and..." ~ Best, Sophie. (2004, September 10). No retread rockers. *The (Melbourne, Australia) Age.*

3. "I think with each record..." ~ Sculley, Alan. (2004, September 17). Black Keys rolling. *The Kansas City Star.*

4. The clip was later ranked... ~ Labate, Steve. (2009, November 9). The 50 best music videos of the decade, 2000-2009. *Paste Magazine.*

5. "We'd done so much overdubbing..." ~ Doyle, Tom. (2014, November). The Black Keys: Pat Carney & Dan Auerbach. *Sound on Sound.*

6. "We hit the fan. It..." ~ Guarino, Mark. (2006, October). Blues brothers. *Harp.*

7. "We aren't making a lot..." ~ Parks, Andrew. (2005, January/February). My city was gone. *Magnet.*

8. "Once we sound-check, we..." ~ Abram, Malcolm X. (2006, June 24). Presenting Pat Carney – on guitar. *The Akron Beacon Journal.*

9. "Listen, it is hard to..." ~ Abdurraqib, Hanif. (2021, May 26). Are the Black Keys still underdogs? *The New York Times Magazine.*

10. "Dan and I ended up..." ~ Soeder, John. (2006, November 17). Duo keeps it simple and familiar, with a definite homey influence. *The Cleveland Plain Dealer.*

CHAPTER 13:

1. "I was worried that no..." ~ Abram, Malcolm X. (2006, February 23). Getting down to their music. *The Akron Beacon Journal.*

2. "We had an idea for..." ~ Abram, Malcolm X. (2006, September 17). The Keys of success. *The Akron Beacon Journal.*

3. "In Akron all basements are..." ~ Doyle, Tom. (2014, November). The Black Keys: Pat Carney & Dan Auerbach. *Sound on Sound.*

4. "We like the sound of..." ~ Anderson, Joan. (2006, October 31). Black Keys retexture the blues. *The Boston Globe.*

5. "I knew of the Black..." ~ Menconi, David. (2013, July 5). Black keys' fame no accident. *The News and Observer.*

6. "Dan Auerbach plays guitar and..." ~ Greene, Andy. (2006, September 21). The Black Keys: *Magic Potion. Rolling Stone.*

7. "Our worst-selling, probably our..." ~ Male, Andrew. (2011, June). Exiles on Main Street. *Mojo.*

CHAPTER 14:

1. "Even when we gave the..." ~ Relic, Peter. (2008, March 6). The Black Keys. *Rolling Stone.*

2. "Brian told us, 'I've got...'" ~ Clayman, Andrew. (2008, October 2). Rubber City roots: The Black Keys 'doggy paddle' from Akron to stardom. *Nashville Scene.*
3. "What we learned most from..." ~ Light, Alan. (2010, December/January). Cold fusion. *Relix.*
4. "I was really excited. I've..." ~ Doyle, Tom. (2014, November). The Black Keys: Pat Carney & Dan Auerbach. *Sound on Sound.*
5. "Brian was very much about..." ~ Perry, Andrew. (2017, August). The *Mojo* interview. *Mojo.*
6. "We were in the middle..." ~ "The Black Keys' journey with fame brings them to the Forum this week." (2014, November 3). *The Los Angeles Daily News.*
7. "spooky, sedate and moody." ~ Talbott, Chris. (2008, April 4). Ike Turner's ghost hovers over Black Keys' latest CD. *The Arizona Sun.*
8. "It's our first tour on..." ~ Proskocil, Niz. (2008, April 10). Success means comfort for the Black Keys. *The Omaha World-Herald.*
9. "What remains remarkable... is how..." ~ Perry, Jonathan. (2008, May 19). Black keys rock the blues in a lean, packed set. *The Boston Globe.*
10. "We've been on eBay, looking..." ~ Soeder, John. (2008, October 8). Dan Auerbach of the Black Keys on 'crazy' tour, homecoming gig. *The Cleveland Plain Dealer.*

CHAPTER 15:
1. "shares DNA with the Keys..." ~ Jones Wright, Lavinia. (2009, February 7). Solo, with soul. *Billboard.*
2. "I had a bunch of..." ~ Tulis, Matt. (2009, September). Roots music: The Black Keys' Dan Auerbach branches out. *Cleveland Magazine.*
3. "I figured my time would..." ~ Soeder, John. (2009, October 23). Following a different drummer, Carney tries bass on the side. *The Cleveland Plain Dealer.*
4. "wiry, hyper guitars and weird..." ~ Hermes, Will. (2009, October 15). Drummer: *Feel Good Together. Rolling Stone.*
5. "I probably should have been..." ~ Swenson, John. (2010, August). Blues brothers. *Relix.*
6. "It was never about, 'Let's...'" ~ Light, Alan. (2010, December/January). Cold fusion. *Relix.*
7. "All the blues music I..." ~ "BlakRoc: The Black Keys do hip-hop." (2009, November 27). *Morning Edition* (NPR).
8. "We weren't trying to make..." ~ Herrera, Monica. (2009, November 28). Blak is the new roc. *Billboard.*
9. "Auerbach – the more verbose, often..." ~ Light, Alan. (2010, December/January). Cold fusion. *Relix.*
10. "We started writing the songs..." ~ Saufley, Charles. (2010, August). Future blues: The Black Keys' Dan Auerbach. *Premier Guitar.*
11. "For the first time, we..." ~ Gill, Andy. (2012, February). Keys to the kingdom. *Uncut.*
12. "I was listening to a..." ~ Saufley, Charles. (2010, August). Future blues: The Black Keys' Dan Auerbach. *Premier Guitar.*

CHAPTER 16:
1. "Pat had gotten divorced, he..." ~ "Album by album." (2013, January). *Uncut.*
2. "[Carney] and his wife were..." ~ Eels, Josh. (2010, May 27). Two against nature. *Rolling Stone.*
3. "[Neill recalled]: 'We talked about...'" ~ Simons, Dave. (2011, August). Mark Neill: Recording the Black Keys at Muscle Shoals. *Sound on Sound.*
4. "He made us take some..." ~ Wake, Matt. (2018, May 18). Keys to success: "Brothers" partially in Muscle Shoals wildly beneficial for both parties. *The Birmingham (Alabama) News.*
5. "was basically like returning to ..." ~ Simpson, Dave. (2021, March). The making of... Tighten Up by the Black Keys. *Uncut.*
6. "We didn't talk about the..." ~ Gill, Andy. (2012, February). Keys to the kingdom. *Uncut.*

7. "Things were happening that were..." ~ Simons, Dave. (2011, August). Mark Neill: Recording the Black Keys at Muscle Shoals. *Sound on Sound*.
8. "We were halfway into it..." ~ Fricke, David. (2020). The Black Keys: *Brothers* [liner notes]. Nonesuch Records.
9. "By the end, I was..." ~ Light, Alan. (2010, December/January). Cold fusion. *Relix*.
10. "We'd never written a hit..." ~ Uhelszki, Jaan. (2019, July). Brothers gonna work it out. *Uncut*.
11. "It was so poppy. We..." ~ Simpson, Dave. (2021, March). The making of... Tighten Up by the Black Keys. *Uncut*.

CHAPTER 17:
1. "Every single friend that went..." ~ Ferris, D.X. (2010, July 21). Brothers in bloom. *Scene*.
2. "[Akron] was just shrinking, shrinking..." ~ Gold, Adam. (2014, December 5). The Black Keys' Pat Carney: The cream interview. *Nashville Scene*.
3. "I felt like hypocrite. Akron's..." ~ Male, Andrew. (2011, June). Exiles on Main Street. *Mojo*.
4. "I'm much happier here, for..." ~ Purcell, Andrew. (2010, July 9). 'It's ridiculous to say that we play the blues.' *The Independent*.
5. "Pat had already left Akron..." ~ Male, Andrew. (2011, June). Exiles on Main Street. *Mojo*.
6. "Right after the flood [in..." ~ Riemenschneider, Chris. (2012, May 13). A new arena for the Black Keys. *The Minneapolis Star Tribune*.
7. "[Ferguson] was one of the..." ~ Blackstock, Peter. (2018, February 8). The wait is over: Dan Auerbach reinvents himself with solo record beyond the Black Keys. *The Austin American-Statesman*.
8. "I didn't want to go..." ~ Fielder, Hugh. (2012, January). Q&A: The Black Keys. *Classic Rock*.
9. "I moved to Nashville... because..." ~ Benson, John. (2018, March 29). Black Keys' Dan Auerbach has solo gig at Agora. *The (Willoughby, OH) News-Herald*.
10. "Pat was living in New..." ~ Diehl, Matt. (2012, April). The Black Keys. *Interview*.
11. "I'm the kind of person..." ~ Uhelszki, Jaan. (2014, July/August). The Black Keys: Chart-topping blues. *Relix*.
12. "a sprawling, almost castlelike stucco..." ~ Doyle, Patrick. (2014, August 11). The dark days behind the Black Keys' best album yet. *Rolling Stone*.
13. "It's kind of interesting that..." ~ Rodgers, D. Patrick. (2011, March 31). Keys to the city: The Black Keys have moved to Nashville. *Nashville Scene*.
14. "Suddenly, old Nashville, has become..." ~ Hemphill, Paul. (1970). *The Nashville Sound*. New York: Simon and Schuster.
15. "It's one of the most..." ~ Battle, Bob. (1976, November). Paul McCartney in Nashville!!! *Country Song Roundup*.

CHAPTER 18:
1. "I imagine Dan and I..." ~ Stewart, Allison. (2010, January 1). Passing time with the Black Keys. *The Chicago Tribune*.
2. "Pat and I have spent..." ~ Eels, Josh. (2010, May 27). Two against nature. *Rolling Stone*.
3. "*Brothers* was classic Muscle Shoals..." ~ Fricke, David. (2020). The Black Keys: *Brothers* [liner notes]. Nonesuch Records.
4. "Our manager told us that..." ~ Simpson, Dave. (2021, March). The making of... Tighten Up by the Black Keys. *Uncut*.
5. "It's like a Laurel and..." ~ Eels, Josh. (2010, May 27). Two against nature. *Rolling Stone*.
6. "Are the Black Keys the..." ~ Sullivan, Matt. (2010, May 17). Are the Black Keys the Best Rock Band in America? *Esquire* [online].
7. "No longer are the Black..." ~ Cridlin, Jay. (2014, December 8). Black Keys' rise to superstardom is complex, messy. *The Tampa Bay Times*.

8. "When things started happening with..." ~ Leahey, Andrew. (2011, November/December). The Black Keys: Brothers in arms. *American Songwriter*.
9. "We used to tour without..." ~ Case, Wesley. (2012, May 18). Rocking on: The Black Keys, the Ohio blues duo, reaches new heights while staying true to its gritty sound. *The Baltimore Sun*.
10. "Mr. Michels and Mr. Movshon..." ~ Chinen, Nate. (2010, July 28). An underground duo finds unfamiliar perch atop the charts. *The New York Times*.
11. "It was perfect conditions for..." ~ Oldham, Tom. (2014, June). To infinity and beyond. *Mojo*.
12. "If you're stressed all the..." ~ White, Ryan. (2014, October 31). The Black Keys refuse to make rock boring. *The Sacramento Bee*.
13. "We're not going to let..." ~ Oshinsky, Matthew. (2009, July 31). Dan Auerbach gets back in black. *The Newark Star-Ledger*.
14. "When no one's buying your..." ~ Hiatt, Brian. (2012, January 19). The rise of the Black Keys: How two Rust Belt refugees became an arena-size, super-charged stomp machine. *Rolling Stone*.
15. "I really always get a..." ~ Si Perna, Alan. (2014, September). Black & Blue. *Guitar World*.
16. "The group gets about one..." ~ Mapes, Jillian. (2012, January 14). Tightened up. *Billboard*.

CHAPTER 19:
1. "We were supposed to go..." ~ Crane, Larry. (2020, April/May). Patrick Carney of the Black Keys. *Tape Op*.
2. "It's like the biggest American..." ~ Heldenfels, Rich. (2011, February 13). TV helps Black keys raise music profile. *The Akron Beacon Journal*.
3. "I remember driving back from..." ~ Diehl, Matt. (2012, April). The Black Keys. *Interview*.
4. "think it's kind of weird..." ~ Rodgers, D. Patrick. (2011, March 31). Keys to the city: The Black Keys have moved to Nashville. *Nashville Scene*.
5. "When we walked the red..." ~ Maerz, Melissa. (2012, January 6. Three rounds with... the Black Keys. *Entertainment Weekly*.
6. "The Black Keys are so..." ~ McCready, John. (2010, June). Structural engineering. *The Word*.
7. "a beacon for hard-hitting..." ~ Scaggs. Austin. (2010, October 28). Q&A: Robert Plant. *Rolling Stone*.
8. "I think Robert Plant and..." ~ Petrusich, Amanda. (2011, January). The Black Keys. *Spin*.
9. "I still think *Brothers* is..." ~ Uhelszki, Jaan. (2019, July). Brothers gonna work it out. *Uncut*.
10. "The lounge also features two..." ~ Doyle, Patrick. (2014, August 11). The dark days behind the Black Keys' best album yet. *Rolling Stone*.
11. "I'm not too picky about..." ~ Drozdowski, Ted. (2012, March). Guitarist Dan Auerbach discusses gear, influences and the latest Black Keys album, *El Camino*. *Guitar World*.
12. "I've got an old piano..." ~ Doyle, Tom. (2014, November). The Black Keys: Pat Carney & Dan Auerbach. *Sound on Sound*.
13. "Having a place that's tailor... ~ Drozdowski, Ted. (2012, March). Guitarist Dan Auerbach discusses gear, influences and the latest Black Keys album, *El Camino*. *Guitar World*.

CHAPTER 20:
1. "I'm sure we felt a..." ~ Masley Ed. (2012, September 30). Rooted in rock & roll. *The Arizona Republic*.
2. "He basically asked if he..." ~ Doyle, Tom. (2012, April). The Black Keys. *Q*.
3. "I mean, it's weird. I've..." ~ Doyle, Tom. (2012, April). The Black Keys. *Q*.
4. "We wanted *El Camino* to..." ~ Micallef, Ken. (2012, January). The Black Keys. *Electronic Musician*.
5. "It was difficult at times..." ~ Kot, Greg. (2012, March 15). Black Keys and their 'rocketship to the moon.' *The Chicago Tribune*.
6. "We were getting into the..." ~ Leahey, Andrew. (2011, November/December). The Black Keys:

Brothers in arms. *American Songwriter*.

7. "This record was way more..." ~ Kot, Greg. (2012, March 15). Black Keys and their 'rocketship to the moon.' *The Chicago Tribune*.

8. "We're all perfectionists, but Brian..." ~ Leahey, Andrew. (2011, November/December). The Black Keys: Brothers in arms. *American Songwriter*.

9. "This is our first pure..." ~ Barracato, Joseph. (2012, January 15). Keys to the city. *The New York Post*.

10. "We've had people say: 'You're..." ~ Simpson, Dave. (2011, December 1). 'We've put in more hours than anyone:' The Black Keys interviewed. *The Guardian*.

11. "It's not the exact van..." ~ Scaggs, Austin. (2011, November 24). Q&A: Dan Auerbach. *Rolling Stone*.

12. "That's the reaction we were..." ~ Abram, Malcolm X. (2011, December 4). Black Keys explode. *The Akron Beacon Journal*.

13. "We let the label pick..." ~ "The Black Keys' journey with fame brings them to the Forum this week." (2014, November 3). *The Los Angeles Daily News*.

14. "Instead of releasing the big-budget..." ~ Mapes, Jillian. (2012, January 14). Tightened up. *Billboard*.

15. "It's accidental if anything. I've..." ~ Barracato, Joseph. (2012, January 15). Keys to the city. *The New York Post*.

16. "They don't make vintage folk-rock..." ~ Maerz, Melissa. (2011, December 2). El Camino review: The Black Keys. *Entertainment Weekly*.

17. "When times are as good as they are on El Camino, the blues can wait for another day." Hyden, Steven. (2011, December 15). The Black Keys: El Camino. The Chicago Tribune.

18. "It's a summer record released..." ~ Roberts, Randall. (2011, December 6). The Black Keys: El Camino. *The Los Angeles Times*.

19. "The Akron, Ohio, guys brought..." ~ Hermes, Will. (2011, December 22). The Keys turn their blues-rock beater into a sleek, shiny muscle car. *Rolling Stone*.

CHAPTER 21:

1. "rock and roll is dying..." ~ Hiatt, Brian. (2012, January 19). The rise of the Black Keys: How two Rust Belt refugees became an arena-size, super-charged stomp machine. *Rolling Stone*.

2. "I mean, look, I've got..." (2012, March). *MTV News*.

3. "Arenas suit the Black Keys, another..." ~ Curtin, Kevin. (2012, May 4). Live shots: The Black Keys. *The Austin Chronicle*.

4. "I think the mainstream public..." ~ Power, Tom. (2012, February 21). The Black Keys' Patrick Carney & Dan Auerbach in Studio Q. *Q With Tom Power* (CBC).

5. "We figured we weren't going..." ~ Talbott, Chris. (2013, February 10). Mumford & Sons, Gotye and Fun. take home Grammys. *The Seattle Times*.

6. "We're going to be playing..." ~ Rogan, Joe. (2019, September 19). Interview with the Black Keys, #1354. *The Joe Rogan Experience* (Spotify podcast).

7. "With regards to the Bieber..." ~ Daniell, Mark. (2014, September 14). Out of the blue: The Black Keys are rocking arenas these days. *The Toronto Sun*.

8. "I think it was very..." ~ Dougherty, Steve. (2012, March 29). Dr. John's unlikely new partner. *The Wall Street Journal*.

9. "He wouldn't commit. I called..." ~ Catchpole, Chris. (2023, April). Let's shop. *Record Collector*.

10. "We were listening to a..." ~ Catchpole, Chris. (2023, April). Let's shop. *Record Collector*.

11. "Black Keys fans coming to..." ~ Empire, Kitty. (2012, March 31). Dr John: *Locked Down* – review. *The Guardian*.

CHAPTER 22:

1. "When you reach a certain..." ~ The Black Keys adjust to bumpy life at the top. (2014, May 31). *The Kokomo Tribune.*
2. "I wasn't even thinking about..." ~ Hiatt, Brian. (2012, January 19). The rise of the Black Keys: How two Rust Belt refugees became an arena-size, super-charged stomp machine. *Rolling Stone.*
3. "We never rehearse, we never..." ~ Murphy, Breanna. (2012, April-May-June). The Black Keys: Same as it ever was. *Filter.*
4. "We went to Michigan to..." ~ Abram, Malcolm. (2014, May 17). Pat Carney of the Black Keys talks about new album, tour. *The Akron Beacon Journal.*
5. "Burton flew home the next..." ~ Doyle, Patrick. (2014, August 11). The dark days behind the Black Keys' best album yet. *Rolling Stone.*
6. "I definitely did not know..." ~ "Concert preview: The Black Keys still moving forward on battered *Turn Blue*." (2014, September 3). *Columbus Alive!*
7. "It was the first time..." ~ Doyle, Patrick. (2014, August 11). The dark days behind the Black Keys' best album yet. *Rolling Stone.*
8. "It was such a relief..." ~ Mathieson, Craig. (2014, September 19). Under lock and Keys. *The Sydney Morning Herald.*
9. "It's not an instantly gratifying..." ~ Hoby, Hermione. (2014, April 26). The Black Keys: Success, depression and divorce. *The Guardian.*
10. "I think all of our..." ~ Abram, Malcolm. (2014, May 17). Pat Carney of the Black Keys talks about new album, tour. *The Akron Beacon Journal.*
11. "Ghoulardi was a great influence, especially..." ~ Petkovic, John. (2013, January 12). Ghoulardi at 50: Tim Conway, Jim Jarmusch, Paul Thomas Anderson pay tribute to Cleveland icon. 'Dead Don't Die.' *The Cleveland Plain Dealer.*
12. "So yeah, if you ask..." ~ Brooks, Xan. (2019, July 7). Jim Jarmusch: 'I'm for the survival of beauty. I'm for the mystery of life. *The Guardian.*
13. "*Turn Blue* is a genuine turning..." ~ Fricke, David. (2014, May 5). *Turn Blue. Rolling Stone.*
14. "*Turn Blue* is soaked in..." ~ Kot, Greg. (2014, May 12). Album review: The Black Keys, *Turn Blue. The Chicago Tribune.*

CHAPTER 23:

1. "We never thought we'd get..." ~ Doyle, Patrick. (2014, August 11). The dark days behind the Black Keys' best album yet. *Rolling Stone.*
2. "We got paid $10, and..." ~ Doyle, Patrick. (2014, October 19). The Black Keys loosen up. *Rolling Stone.*
3. "He gave me some confidence..." ~ Droppo, Dana (2014, July). Lana Del Rey interview: Against the grain. *Complex.*
4. "Her songs were so strong..." ~ Oldham, Tom. (2014, June). To infinity and beyond. *Mojo.*
5. "With Lana, that was the..." ~ Uhelszki, Jaan. (2018, May). Dan Auerbach: "I don't think I'm that much of a control freak any more..." *Uncut.*
6. "Producer Dan Auerbach, of the..." ~ Puckett, Lee. (2014, June 16). Lana Del Rey carves out her own place in pop. *The Louisville Courier Journal.*
7. "Playing against a backdrop designed..." ~ "Concert review: The Black Keys at the Schottenstein Center." (2014, September 6). *Columbus Alive!*
8. "The Pretenders sounded awesome and..." ~ Abram, Malcolm X. (2014, September 4). A Black Key comes home: An interview with drummer Patrick Carney. *The Canton Repository.*
9. "I like it, but I..." ~ Abram, Malcolm X. (2014, September 4). A Black Key comes home: An interview with drummer Patrick Carney. *The Canton Repository.*
10. "There are kids at school..." ~ Weiner, Jonah. (2014, June 5). The great White way. *Rolling Stone.*
11. "I was pretty surprised by..." ~ Uhelszki, Jaan. (2014, July/August). The Black Keys: Chart-

topping blues. *Relix*.

12. "I got into music because..." ~ Unnamed representative of Patrick Carney. (2015, September). Statement.

CHAPTER 24:

1. "This is not a side-project..." ~ Gold, Adam. (2015, September 17). Black Keys frontman Dan Auerbach tells us about his funky new band, the record he made with his dad and more. *The Nashville Scene*.
2. "He's ballsy, man. He set..." ~ Gold, Adam. (2015, September 17). Black Keys frontman Dan Auerbach tells us about his funky new band, the record he made with his dad and more. *The Nashville Scene*.
3. "On Friday, the Black Keys..." ~ Beaumont, Mark. (2015, June 14). Isle of Wight Festival 2015 – review. *The Guardian*.
4. "When we tell people that..." ~ Vozick-Levinson, Simon. (2015, September 10). Q&A: Dan Auerbach. *Rolling Stone*.
5. "We'd been caged up together..." ~ Paulson, Dave. (2019, July 17). Duo finds renewal after hiatus, inspiration in an unlikely spot. The *Tennessean*.
6. "It was fun going on..." ~ Yarborough, Chuck. (2019, September 25). Black Keys say 'Let's Rock' with new album and a visit to Rocket Mortgage FieldHouse. *The Cleveland Plain Dealer*.
7. "We're absolutely record geeks and..." ~ Abram, Malcolm X. (2015, December 3). For the Arcs, it's unusual and familiar at the same time. *The Akron Beacon Journal*.
8. "There were like 40 songs..." ~ Hall, Kristin M. (2015, September 6). Dan Auerbach fronts new band the Arcs for diverse sound. *The St. Louis Post-Dispatch*.
9. "Leon [Michels] and I were in..." ~ Durchholz, Daniel. (2016, April 22). Pleasant dreams. *The St. Louis Post-Dispatch*.
10. "We're still doing some figuring..." ~ Abram, Malcolm X. (2015, December 3). For the Arcs, it's unusual and familiar at the same time. *The Akron Beacon Journal*.
11. "They approached me about producing..." ~ Bandyke, Martin. (2015, December 3). Five questions for Dan Auerbach, Black Keys guitarist and vocalist. *The Detroit Free Press*.
12. "We thought Dan was really..." ~ Knopper, Steve. (2016, December 2). Effort to simplify boosts Cage the Elephant's sound. *The Chicago Tribune*.
13. "While I thoroughly enjoy the..." ~ Pfrommer, Jason. (2015, November 12). Too much Back Keys in Cage the Elephant track. *The Northwest Herald*.
14. "I tend to gravitate towards..." ~ Graff, Gary. (2020, June 29). Q&A with the Black Keys. *Music Connection*.
15. "I was nervous. I have..." ~ Beaven, Michael. (2016, April 6). First pitch is ball for Akron rocker: Black Keys' Patrick Carney makes a ceremonial throw for Tribe. *The Akron Beacon Journal*.
16. "He had no idea who..." ~ Newman, Jason. (2016, April 13). Black Keys: We regret inducting Steve Miller after Rock Hall insults. *Rolling Stone* [online].
17. "I wrote one line of..." ~ Niesel, Jeff. (2019, September 25). A rejuvenated Black Keys. *Scene*.
18. "I think their experience was..." ~ Waddell, Ray. (2016, April 15). 'Nice Guy' Steve Miller talks Rock Hall Rancor, who he wishes had inducted him and how he'd fix the whole 'rude' process. *Billboard*.
19. "I wanted to ask Elton..." ~ Waddell, Ray. (2016, April 15). 'Nice Guy' Steve Miller talks Rock Hall Rancor, who he wishes had inducted him and how he'd fix the whole 'rude' process. *Billboard*.

CHAPTER 25:

1. "When I was 17, I'd..." ~ Meeker, Ward. (2019, October). Dan Auerbach: Black (Keys) magic. *Vintage Guitar*.

2. "Like Hendrix and the Who..." ~ Francis, Thomas. (2004, December 8). Lord of the strings. *Scene*.
3. "He was my guitar hero..." ~ Graff, Gary. (2020, July). Black Keys. *Music Connection*.
4. "I had Glenn [in] the..." ~ Meeker, Ward. (2019, October). Dan Auerbach: Black (Keys) magic. *Vintage Guitar*.
5. "He's on such a roll..." ~ Fragassi, Selena. (2016, November 30). Chrissie Hynde happy to return to Pretenders 'Alone.' *The Chicago Sun-Times*.
6. "I never met him in..." ~ Bienstock, Richard. (2016, November). Chrissie Hynde on teaming with Dan Auerbach & the 'bullsh-t' of 'Grammy culture.' *Billboard*.
7. "I got there, it was..." ~ Bienstock, Richard. (2016, November). Chrissie Hynde on teaming with Dan Auerbach & the 'bullsh-t' of 'Grammy culture.' *Billboard*.
8. "The first day we were... ~ Bienstock, Richard. (2016, November). Chrissie Hynde on teaming with Dan Auerbach & the 'bullsh-t' of 'Grammy culture.' *Billboard*.
9. "All of my songs are..." ~ Fragassi, Selena. (2016, November 30). Chrissie Hynde happy to return to Pretenders 'Alone.' *The Chicago Sun-Times*.
10. "I wrote most of these..." ~ Lewis, John. (2016, November). Alone. *Uncut*.
11. "Recording with Chrissie was great. She's..." ~ Drozdowski, Ted. (2017, February). Kenny Vaughan and Dave Roe: Inside the *Alone* sessions. *Premiere Guitar*.

CHAPTER 26:
1. "I felt like I had..." ~ Perry, Andrew. (2017, August). The *Mojo* interview. *Mojo*.
2. "When I was growing up..." ~ Wood, James. (2017, June). Black Keys' Dan Auerbach talks new solo album, 'Waiting On a Song.' *Guitar World*.
3. "Sometimes I feel like I..." ~ Jones, Sarah. (2017, August). Dan Auerbach. *Electronic Musician*.
4. "That was a strange one..." ~ Meeker, Ward. (2017, August). Dan Auerbach: Nashville collaborative. *Vintage Guitar*.
5. "[Auerbach] put me in his..." ~ Wilson, Lois. (2018, January). Robert Finley. *Mojo*.
6. "She changed my life. We..." ~ Riemenschneider, Chris. (2019, September 27). Back in Black Keys. *The Minneapolis Star Review*.
7. "Watching him make music was..." ~ Petkovic, John. (2017, December 18). Ralph Carney, renowned Akron native musician. *The Cleveland Plain Dealer*.

CHAPTER 27:
1. "I was destined to do..." ~ Yarborough, Chuck. (2018, March 30). Finding his muse in Music City, Auerbach is happily producing. *The Cleveland Plain Dealer*.
2. "We're both just sort of..." ~ Riemenschneider, Chris. (2019, September 27). Back in Black Keys. *The Minneapolis Star Review*.
3. "We had kind of just..." ~ Graff, Gary. (2020, June 29). Q&A with the Black Keys. *Music Connection*.
4. "Looking at some of our..." ~ Stewart, Allison. (2019, September 26. Patrick Carney doesn't believe in reunions either, so the Black Keys are back after a break. *The Chicago Tribune*.
5. "I knew we were going..." ~ Pareles, Jon. (2019, June 27). For the Black Keys, rock lives. It just had to wait. *The New York Times*.
6. "We didn't even talk about..." ~ Meeker, Ward. (2019, October). Dan Auerbach: Black (Keys) magic. *Vintage Guitar*.
7. "We've only worked with one..." ~ Daniell, Mark. (2019, October 6). Back in black: Patrick Carney talks Black Keys comeback, realizing his rock dreams and why he always gets to choose the first and last song at every show they play. *The Toronto Sun*.
8. "I was reading *The Tennessean*..." ~ Piya, Sinha-Roy. (2019, July 5). The Black Keys. *Entertainment Weekly*.
9. "We've both been playing a..." ~ Benson, John. (2019, September 27). Akron-bred Black Keys

return with ninth album. *The Elyria Chronicle-Telegram.*

10. "We realized that we didn't..." ~ Pareles, Jon. (2019, June 27). For the Black Keys, rock lives. It just had to wait. *The New York Times.*

11. "It's a big step down..." ~ Zaillian, Charlie. (2019, September 26). The Black Keys are back, and keeping things in proportion. *Nashville Scene.*

12. "During the COVID year, I..." ~ Price, Mark J. (2021, May 14). Informal sessions in late-2019 after completing an album for Louisiana singer-songwriter Robert Finley. *The Akron Beacon Journal.*

CHAPTER 28:

1. "I called Pat up, and..." ~ Barton, Laura. (2021, May 16). Blues brothers. *The Independent.*

2. "If it weren't for this..." ~ Price, Mark. (2021, May 14). Informal sessions in late-2019 after completing an album for Louisiana singer-songwriter Robert Finley. *The Akron Beacon Journal.*

3. "Yeah, there's probably zero commercial..." ~ Himes, Geoffrey. (2021, May 20. The Black Keys acknowledge their muses on Delta Kream. *Nashville Scene.*

4. "Dan's dad asked me, 'Where..." ~ Daniell, Mark. (2020, December 25). Oh brothers: The Black Keys celebrate 10 years of their Grammy-winning album. *The Windsor Star.*

5. "We definitely made our name... ~ Dansby, Andrew. (2022, October 11). Black Keys 'Drop Out' with new album, drop in on Houston. *The Houston Chronicle.*

6. "Are the Black Keys still..." ~ Abdurraqib, Hanif. (2021, May 26). Are the Black Keys still underdogs? *The New York Times Magazine.*

7. "I got over there with..." ~ Hall, Kristin M. (2022, June 17). Hank Jr. unleashes Thunderhead Hawkins on bawdy blues record. *The San Diego Union-Tribune.*

8. "Auerbach's biggest contribution may have..." ~ Specker, Lawrence. (2022, June 28). Hank Jr. has the blues – the 'Rich White Honky Blues,' to be specific. *The Birmingham News.*

CHAPTER 29:

1. "Some of the songs are..." ~ Masley, Ed. (2022, October 5). Dan Auerbach shares the 'magic trick we learned at 16' that keeps the Black Keys going. *The Arizona Republic.*

2. "The whole Billy F. Gibbons..." ~ Nickoloff, Annie. (2022, July 27). The Black Keys' Dan Auerbach went from Blossom Music Center parking attendant to headliner (Q&A). *The Cleveland Plain Dealer.*

3. "He didn't bring a guitar..." ~ Graff, Gary. (2022, September 6). Black Keys at Pine Knob Music Theatre, 5 things to know. *The Oakland Press.*

4. "That's us playing... with no..." ~ Benson, John. (2022, September 9). The Black Keys are back in Northeastern Ohio tonight. *The Elyria Chronicle-Telegraph.*

5. "I bought it off of..." ~ Derdeyn, Stuart. (2022, September 27). Q&A: Black Keys' Dan Auerbach not singing the blues on new album Dropout Boogie. *The Vancouver Sun.*

6. "a refreshing dash of bubblegum..." ~ Davenport, Rich; Elliott, Paul; Everley, Dave; et al. (2023, January). Albums of 2022. *Classic Rock.*

7. "Dan's daughter's in high school..." ~ Greenblatt, Leah. (2022, May 13). The Black Keys on the Kmart pomade, dirt weed, and haunted tire factories that shaped their sound. *Entertainment Weekly* [online].

8. "I've never experienced anything like..." ~ Greene, Alex. (2022, September 29). Greg Cartwright opens up about songwriting and his hit Black Keys co-writer. *Memphis Flyer.*

9. "Sometimes I think that would..." ~ Catchpole, Chris. (2023, April). Let's shop. *Record Collector.*

10. "I have two little kids..." ~ Gavin, Christopher. (2022, July 18). The Black Keys' Pat Carney on 'Dropout Boogie,' going back on tour, and the 'small world' of rock 'n' roll. *The Boston Globe.*

11. "We're both just totally addicted..." ~ Masley, Ed. (2022, October 5). Dan Auerbach shares the 'magic trick we learned at 16' that keeps the Black Keys going. *The Arizona Republic.*

EPILOGUE

1. "We were just flying by... ~ Paulson, Dave. (2021, May 21). The Black Keys rediscover their blues roots, 20 years later. *The Chillicothe Gazette*.
2. "I mean, Akron's always home..." ~ Joy, Kevin. (2014, August 31). Keys signature. *The Columbus Dispatch*.
3. "Well, we will always be..." ~ Rodgers, D. Patrick. (2011, March 31). Keys to the city: The Black Keys have moved to Nashville. *Nashville Scene*.
4. "We're both very, very appreciative..." ~ Appleton, Rory. (2022, July 12). Black Keys' Patrick Carney on the band's mentality, upcoming tour and Indy memories. *The Indianapolis Star*.
5. "I think our relationship would..." ~ Diehl, Matt. (2012, April). The Black Keys. *Interview*.

▶ INDEX

New York City, 5, 23, 26-27, 30, 32, 58, 71, 92, 98-99, 131, 134, 143
The New York Times, 36, 104
Newman, Laraine, 107
Nickelback, 121
Nine Inch Nails, 164
Nissan, 105
No Reservations, 118
Nonesuch Records, 74, 83, 129
Northside Lounge, 40, 41
The Numbers Band (15-60-75), 11, 33
N.W.A., 41

O
Oasis, 168
Oberlin, Ohio, 23
Odenkirk, Bob, 116
Ohio & Erie Canal, 1
Ohio River, 1
The Ohio State University, 25
Ohio Turnpike, 108
Ohio University, 25
One Way Rider, 79
O'Neil's department store, 6
Optigan, 167
Orange, 16
Osbourne, Ozzy, 168
Oxford, Mississippi, 59

P
Pacific Gas & Electric, 146
Painesville, Ohio, 78
Pappy Van Winkle bourbon, 118
Paramount Theater, 5
The Party of Helicopters, 22, 70
Paste magazine, 69
Patton, Charley, 109
Patty Darling, 23
Pearl Jam, 71-72

Peel, John, 64
Peets, John, 106
Pere Ubu, 78, 129
Peter Gunn TV show, 5
Petkovic, John, 159
Petraglia, Angelo, 167
Pilgrimage Festival, 165
The Pilgrims, 145
Pink Floyd, 117
Pitchfork, 135
Pizza Hut, 106
Plant, Robert, 109-110
Polsky's department store, 6
Portage Hotel, 2
Portland, Oregon, 56
The Preservation Hall Jazz Band, 122
Presley, Elvis, 5, 100, 157
The Pretenders, 7, 58, 141, 149
Prine, John, 98, 138, 151
ProTools, 77-78

Q
Q: Are We Not Men? A: We Are Devo!, 16
Q Prime Nashville, 106
Q-Tip, 86
Quicken Loans Arena, 131
Quine, Robert, 30-32
Quine, Rosalie, 32
Quine, Tim, 42
Quonset Hut, 39

R
The Raconteurs, 97
Radio Shack, 52
Radiohead, 71
Raekwon, 86, 109
Rain Dogs, 14
The Rawboogie, 41
Ray, Nicole, 86

▶ PHOTO CREDITS

Cover – Image Press Agency / depositphotos.com.
Page 4 – Author's collection.
Page 9 – Author's collection.
Page 21 – Author's collection.
Page 33 – Author's collection.
Page 37 – Photographs in the Ben May Charitable Trust Collection of Mississippi. Photographs in the Carol M. Highsmith Archive, Library of Congress, Prints and Photographs Division.
Page 49 – Author's collection.
Page 53 – Author's collection.
Page 55 – Author's collection.
Page 69 – Author's collection.
Page 80 – Author's collection.
Page 81 – Author's collection.
Page 84 – Author's collection.
Page 91 – The George F. Landegger Collection of Alabama Photographs in Carol M. Highsmith's America, Library of Congress, Prints and Photographs Division.
Page 96 – Author's collection.
Page 97 – The George F. Landegger Collection of Alabama Photographs in Carol M. Highsmith's America, Library of Congress, Prints and Photographs Division.
Page 116 – Author's collection.
Page 138 – Author's collection.
Page 148 – Courtesy of John Mascolo.

I owe a debt of gratitude to following individuals: John Mascolo, Mary Ellen Huesken, Mike Olszewski, Jon Mosey, Harvey Gold, Sigmund Vaccaro, Ben Fulkman, Danny Basone, the late Al Kerkian of Sarah's Deli and the late Bob Bingham of the Baseliners. I am also grateful to all of the individuals who consented to my interview requests.

Printed in the USA
CPSIA information can be obtained
at www.ICGtesting.com
LVHW060937271123
764988LV00066B/2306